"Dream as if you'll live forever. Live as if you'll die today.
The gratification comes in the doing, not in the results."

*James Dean*

# Contents

**Publisher:** Reinhard Klein
**Editor:** Colin McMaster
**Authors:** David Evans & Colin McMaster
**Design and layout:** Ellen Böhle-Hanigk
**Coordination:** Sarah Vessely
**Editorial staff:** Daniel Klein, Sebastian Klein

**Photography:** All photography from the McKlein archive (comprising the works of: Reinhard Klein, Bob McCaffrey, Colin McMaster, Tony Welam, Hugh Bishop, Ross Hyde, Colin Taylor Productions, Jakob Ebrey, Darren Heath) Other images: LAT Photographic (p.4, 7, 11, 22, 23, 25, 29, 30, 31, 34, 38, 44, 46, 49, 52, 54, 73, 78, 90, 101, 102, 131, 182-183, 194, 199, 214-215, 218, 225, 234-235, 241, 248, 250, 251), Robert Griffin (p. 8), McRae Family archive (p. 14, 15, 18, 19, 24, 134), Tom Coffield Snr. (p. 20-21, 26-27, 29, 35), Tony Walker (p. 26), Maurice Seldon (p. 32), Les Kolczak (p. 32, 33, 41), Mark Bothwell (p. 50), Bryn Williams (p. 51), Alan McGuiness (p. 60, 100, 101, 135, 242), Pernilla Solberg (p. 121), North One Television (p. 169), Julian Porter (p. 192), Esteban Delgado (p. 198, 247), Nissan (p. 216), Richard Thompson (p. 219, 222, 223), Roy Dempster (p. 224, 228-229, 230), Chris Yandell - Vermont Subaru USA (p. 231, 236-237, 237)

**Special thanks to:** The McRae family: Jim, Margaret, Alister, Stuart, Alison & Hollie; Markku Alén, Autosport magazine, Jim Bamber, Ken Block, Mike Broad, Garry Connelly, David Coulthard, Sandra Evans, Anne Fitzpatrick, Dario Franchitti, Alexander Galitzki, Fred Gallagher, Nicky Grist, Andy Hallbery, Daniel Klein, Reinhard Klein, Sebastian Klein, Ursula Kleinmanns, David Lapworth, Jari-Matti Latvala, Barrie Lochhead, Barry Lock, Sébastien Loeb, Christian Loriaux, Ari Mantyla, Tommi Mäkinen, Marko Märtin, Alan McGuiness, Andrea McMaster, Jenny McMaster, Kris Meeke, Luis Moya, Matt Neal, Luis Podenco, Robert Reid, David Richards CBE, Nigel Riddle, Derek Ringer, Marie-Pierre Rossi, Carlos Sainz, Angus Scott, Phil Short, Petter Solberg, Tina Thörner, Darren Turner, Sarah Vessely, Martin Wilkinson, Malcolm Wilson OBE, Kevin Wood

**Reproductions:** McKlein Publishing
**Printing:** Himmer AG, Augsburg, Germany
**Distribution:** RallyWebShop (www.rallywebshop.com)

**Copyright:**
McKlein Publishing/Verlag Reinhard Klein & Ursula Kleinmanns GbR
Hauptstr. 172
51143 Cologne
Germany
Tel.: +49-(0)2203-359239
Fax: +49-(0)2203-359238
publishing@mcklein.de
www.mckleinstore.com
www.mcklein.de

1st edition — 2013
ISBN-13: 978-3-927458-64-2

**Imprint**

# Foreword
## by Alister McRae

Coming out of the Pundershaw stage on the 1995 RAC, Colin and Derek were working on their Subaru at the side of the road. There had been a problem, a puncture. I asked my co-driver Chris [Wood] what their time was. They'd dropped two minutes.

"Hmm," I said, "that's a pretty tall order that. Taking two minutes back on Carlos …"

Winning the championship was everything they had been working towards and it was looking a bit shaky.

Colin always had a self-belief that, from A to B, he could be quicker than anyone; that's one of the things that made him who he was. When I saw him before the start of the next stage his answer to the two minutes was: "She'll be fine. No problem."

That was Colin. He wasn't going to give up. Winning was everything for him. It just meant he was going to do it the hard way. Or, for Colin, the most enjoyable way: flat out!

He'd never been any different. Ever since we were kids in the back garden, racing around on our bikes. He'd give anything to beat me and I'd be right back at him.

I don't really have a first memory of Colin, being an older brother – he was two years up on me – he was just always there. We were always good friends as brothers. Of course there were the usual brotherly fights, but none too serious that we wouldn't be back to our usual testing of our Mum's nerves with our next bike jumping competition fairly quickly. I'm sure most of our mates in the street thought we were a bit daft!

Our friendship got stronger and stronger as we got older – especially when it came to motorbikes and then cars. Obviously, Colin was driving on the road before me and we had some good times then. There were a few scrapes in those early years, but I don't remember too many incidents that I would talk about!

I definitely wasn't involved in timing my Dad's Vauxhall HA van through Coalburn Forest and I didn't distract my Grandad so Colin and Robbie could push the Prodrive 911 recce car down the drive and out of sight before starting it and heading off for a bit of a test!

Basically if it had an engine, the only option was to see how fast it would go.

I was away when Colin did his first rally. We all were. I think our younger brother Stuart and I had been forced to go to Spain with Mum and Dad. Colin, being that bit older, had been allowed to stay home alone.

He and some of the boys from Coltness Car Club got a car sorted – a Hillman Avenger – and they were away to Kames for Colin's first event, without Mum and Dad even knowing about it.

I do remember the first event with the Sunbeam. I was spectating with Dad in the forest. As is always the case, the cars were getting slower and slower as the numbers went by. And then you could hear this thing singing through the woods. Dad said: "That's more like it, someone's going for it…"

He was smiling and saying: "This is going to be good." And then this Sunbeam came into view, half in the ditch and fully sideways. Dad's face changed pretty quickly when he saw it was Colin!

Colin was always ready to help when we were both early in our careers. He loaned me his Nova and co-drove for me on my first gravel event. I reckon it was just to make sure I didn't crash his car. It was one of the few times he sat with me. I remember him getting a bit frustrated as he gave me some pointers and I wasn't listening. In the end he got in and drove the next stage. I got it then… "Ah, you mean like that!"

When we swapped back over, I reckoned I had it sussed. Now he was trying to slow me down rather than egg me on. The speed was there but maybe the skill wasn't!

It wasn't all plain sailing for Colin and I in our early careers. Mum and Dad were quite clear that if we wanted something then we had to work for it, and that was how it went in rallying as well. Definitely, there were some people who thought we had been handed things on a bit of a plate and, OK, there's no doubt the McRae name helped. Dad did all he could to put deals together and help with sponsorship, but when it came down to it, we had to do the driving.

Colin's attitude to all that kind of stuff was pretty straightforward. He would just get on and drive. His attitude was straightforward: "You've got what you've got, now get in it and drive it faster. You know what you've got to do: beat all the other guys."

Once Colin got into the Subaru, it was clear that the first win was coming soon. When it did come, in New Zealand, I think it was even more impressive that it came somewhere so far from home, so far from the UK rally scene. Colin had really taken on the world and beaten them.

It didn't make it very easy to keep up with though. There were no iPhones around in 1993! I was at home in Scotland when the rally

was on. I remember being over at Robbie Head's house. We'd been to the pub for a few beers before settling down for the night to try and keep in touch with the other side of the world. There was plenty to celebrate that night – or day as it turned out. And there would be more to come.

The RAC in 1994 was great, but it was the following year which really sticks in my memory. That party in Chester in 1995 was a proper party. It was the perfect end to the perfect year. I was British Champion and finished fourth on the RAC behind the three Subarus and Colin was World Champion. There were more than a few sore heads the morning after!

One thing I would love to have done is to share a team with Colin for a season or two. That would have been perfect for both of us, although I'm sure the team manager would have had a few headaches with it. I think, for Dad, it couldn't have gotten any better than that.

We did drive together on the 1998 RAC, when I joined the Subaru team. It was great. There was fair bit of pre-event hype, but the best part was getting the opportunity to work together. Colin came in the car with me at the final test. He knew that car inside out and was able to confirm what I was thinking as far as set up and getting the most out of what was a new car to me.

There are always some nerves before any rally, but that event was a big chance for me at a big point in my career, so there were the full

nerves before that one. I'll never forget the first stage. Colin and I set exactly the same time, to the tenth of a second. That settled the nerves nicely. Unfortunately, the rally didn't end the way either of us would have liked. And it was, of course, Colin's last rally with Subaru.

It was clear at that time that Colin was ready to move on, ready for the next challenge. And that challenge was at Ford. There was a lot of talk around the time about the money Colin was going to be paid to drive the Focus. The money was nice, but it wasn't what motivated Colin – he wanted to be the best. He wanted to be world champion again. That's not to say the money wasn't important, of course it was, but not in a material way. The money established a pecking order among the drivers and, having taken quite a step up in salary, Colin was at the top of the list.

To win the Safari and Portugal rallies started the relationship with Ford perfectly. They were two completely different wins. The Safari was one of Colin's best, but probably in a way not usually associated with his driving. He almost nursed the car through the event and only did enough to win without risking breaking what was a very new car. Portugal was back to his flat out best. I remember chatting to him before the first stage. He had been discussing tyre options with the team and they were recommending the soft compound tyre and play it in gently but Colin wanted the medium and was going to put it all on the line, maximum attack. His idea was to catch them napping, which he did and went on to win. There were

plenty of wins but, unfortunately, the years at Ford didn't produce another championship.

It's fair to say that when the end of Colin's [WRC] career came in 2003, he wasn't ready for it. He didn't want to stop and there would always be a bit of regret that he hadn't stopped on his own terms. There would always be some unfinished business. I remember in the middle of 2007, Colin was on the phone talking about going back to Subaru. He was excited about the possibility of being back where it all started and back working with David Richards, who had given him the break back at the start.

At the same time, Colin had definitely moved into a different time in his life. I know from personal experience that when you've been in the world championship and constantly on the move, it does come as a bit of a culture shock not to be doing it. The excitement, adrenalin and the satisfaction you get from driving is very hard to match. Colin seemed to have relaxed into it though. He was really loving that time of his life with Alison, Hollie and Johnny. I think he had settled down and was ready for the next chapter.

I'm living in Australia now with my family, but I'll always be Scottish and I'll always be a McRae. I've had some success of my own with the British and Asia-Pacific Championship titles, but to nine out of 10 people, I'm always going to be Colin's brother. A very good friend of mine, and Colin's, said that if I ever wrote a book he had the perfect title: "Living in the shadow."

As a brother and best mate, I've got mountains of great memories of Colin. So being under the shadow wasn't so bad!

# Introduction
## Colin McMaster

A poetic ballet, sideways at 100mph on gravel, mud, snow and tar. Fearsome drops, cliff faces, ravines, trees and passionate fans encroaching onto the road. Waltzing between all this, rally drivers push man and machine to the limit, it's a job that borders on insanity at times. Colin McRae was one of the best rally drivers the world has ever seen. His natural talent and flamboyant style behind the wheel turned him into a global superstar, he could make a car dance. Entertainment through speed was in his DNA and his audience, the world over, loved him for that. He was one of the finest men I ever met, totally down to earth, had a great sense of humour and was extremely generous with both his time and money. Colin McRae was my friend.

I was eight years old when I had my first encounter with the McRae DNA. It happened on the 1978 Scottish Rally, through a bizarre meeting of our fathers. Mine, Bill McMaster, helped push Colin's, Jimmy McRae, out of the woods after his Vauxhall Chevette slid off opposite the McMaster family. It wasn't until 1992 before my next McRae encounter. The meeting place was inside Colin's Subaru rally car, where I was strapped-in next to the man himself, to do a pre-RAC rally photo-shoot for Rothmans.

Quite a lot had happened to both Colins in the intervening 14 years. We had both grown up in Scotland, and we both entered our respective family 'businesses'. Life as a plumber however wasn't for Colin McRae. Resourcefully McRae Jnr worked his way through the lower echelons of rallying, emerging as the brightest British talent in the sport for decades. Prodrive (running the Subaru World Rally Team) signed him on a professional contract in 1991 and he immediately repaid their faith by winning the British Championship. By the end of 1992 the world was calling for McRae Jnr.

For myself, I loved motorsport and I was keen to follow my grandfather's footsteps into a career in the motoring press. My first love was for photography and I married together my passions by taking a job at an Oxford based media agency called Words & Pictures. By 1992 I had fulfilled something of a lifetime ambition by making it into F1, travelling the world photographing the Grands Prix. Geography was in my favour because Prodrive's press and public relations manager Belinda Jellett's commute to work in Banbury took her past the doorstep of Words & Pictures. Prodrive needed a photographer to support their creative PR campaign of Colin McRae and that job became mine soon after Belinda knocked on the door. The 1992 RAC rally was on the horizon and I had my first job, and meeting, with the rally driver who would become my hero.

It didn't take long for success to come for both Colins. I had the dream job I always wanted and Colin had a world championship in his pocket, both by our mid-20s. We had become good friends and would sometimes go out for dinner in the days before a WRC rally. When my wife Andrea came to Rally Australia in 2000, Colin rang me on the Monday morning after the rally to invite us to join him for a boat cruise along Perth's Swan river. The boat was huge, a gin palace, and the lunch stop was epic. We enjoyed several seafood courses and fine wines, amid excellent company. McRae was in his element when he convinced Andrea that the wasabi cube on her scallop plate was in fact avocado, and should be swallowed whole. When the bill came the McRae credit card came out immediately, Colin loved treating his friends.

Colin and I had a great working relationship, McKlein Photography being contracted by both Subaru and Ford. In the early days McRae was ill at ease in front of the camera but he trusted me and knew that if I ever asked him to pose for a specific photograph then I would make him look good. Our finest moments came when Colin had a steering wheel in his hands, doing what he did best. While out scouting for good photo locations on the 1998 Tour de Corse, I found an old stone humpback bridge. Unfortunately, the bridge wasn't on a competitive stage, but instead on a public road liaison section. If driven at speed a rally car would easily take off on the bridge. So I asked Colin and Nicky Grist if they would stop before the bridge, put their helmets on and then jump over the bridge. Colin thought this would look great and said, "Aye, nae bother McMaster – just make sure you're there with your camera." We both kept our sides of the deal.

In Portugal 1997 I set up an in-car camera to shoot Colin and Nicky at work. They drove off for a run with the camera firing automatically every ten seconds and when they returned they couldn't stop laughing. They wouldn't share the joke with me and it wasn't until days later when I had the film processed that all became clear. Among some other funnies, they'd pulled 'the bird' to the camera. I had that picture framed and it has hung on my office wall ever since. *Rally XS* magazine ran a Colin McRae feature in 2001, where Colin selected his favourite rally photos of all time and made comments about them. For the in-car shot in Portugal he said: "I remember this shoot. It was in Portugal, with Colin McMaster. That was for him, that one! We'd had to do a normal run so we decided to have a bit of fun as well."

Good photography is all about standing in the right place at the right time. In this respect Colin made my job easier, providing great action photos pretty much everywhere. More often than not, he would jump the highest, make the biggest splash and slide a car at wider angles than the others. His all-out attacking driving style won him global adulation; everybody who ever saw him drive retains a memory of the experience. My own favourite McRae moment was in Australia, on the renowned jumps at the end of the Bunnings stage. Colin always attacked the crests flat-out, perhaps simply as a crowd-pleasing gesture? The image of his blue and yellow Subaru pointing skywards at Bunnings has passed into WRC folklore and, of course, features within this book.

But it wasn't all a banquets and bouquets. McRae was prone to occasional displays of youthful petulance and it was not unknown for the odd toy to part company with his pram. Colin was fair, he played by the rules, but if things didn't go his way then the rules were often 'stupid'. He didn't do team orders. This perennial thorny motorsport subject reared its ugly head in Catalunya, 1995, and Colin reacted strongly. In sport it is important to know how to lose as well as how to win, however no professional sportsman takes kindly to being ordered to lose. When asked to do just that in Spain, Colin spat out his dummy.

There were many times when Colin found himself under enormous pressure, but he had the coolness and ability to make driving fast look easy. He could handle pressure. If winning a fiercely fought rally depended on a final stage battle between drivers, then more often than not Colin would come out on top. There was nobody better in a one-on-one fight for victory. The record books say Colin McRae won 25 WRC rallies and one World Championship. McRae's legacy is not about statistics, it's about the excitement, passion and flair he brought to the sport of rallying. Colin never properly adapted his style to suit the later World Rally Cars that rewarded straighter, less

sideways driving. Essentially Colin was an entertainer, it was in his nature and I'm not sure he would ever have changed his approach.

I started writing this book in 2010, three years before final publication. It has not been an easy ride. Like a good rally stage there have been some bumps and difficult sections along the way. By the end of 2012, I felt I was going round in circles without moving forwards. Just when I contemplated shelving the project a bright light appeared at the end of the tunnel, in the form of David Evans. Without David's help with the words, this book would never have been finished.

The goal from the outset was to publish the ultimate true portrait of the most celebrated rally driver ever, "McRae, just Colin." I spoke at length to those that knew Colin best, people who worked with him, friends and rivals. I would like to thank all those who gave up their time to share their best memories, in particular his two main co-drivers Derek Ringer and Nicky Grist. These two men spent the most time with Colin, from the best view in the house. I am also extremely grateful to the McRae family for all the help and assistance they have provided. 35 years after that 1978 Scottish Rally, I was back pretty much where it all started for me, Scotland. David Evans and I spent many hours in the company of Jimmy, Margaret, Stuart, Alison and Hollie McRae, just reminiscing. At times tears were shed, however the overwhelming emotions were ones of fun and laughter as we all retold our stories and anecdotes of Colin and Johnny.

Finally I owe some special personal thanks to some special people. To my loving family, who constantly put up with their patriarch's nomadic lifestyle, chasing the WRC around the globe. To my mother Jenny, a retired schoolteacher, who was put to back to work with some proofreading. Finally, to my late father Bill, the man that inspired and encouraged me to follow my passions into a career in motorsport. A job that enabled me to meet, work and play with Colin McRae.

# Introduction
## David Evans

Most 15-year-olds meet somebody who will help shape their life. I met Colin. And I met him at scrutineering in Cardiff for the 1988 Fram Welsh Rally. He was leaning on his Vauxhall Nova. My first conversation was one I'll never forget. I suspect he might have forgotten it pretty quickly.

"Can I have your autograph, please?"

Now, to engage him further… "Where's your Dad?"

"He's stuck in traffic on his way here."

Err… That was it. I had nothing more to offer. I left Colin leaning.

But, from then on, I was transfixed and followed his career religiously. My father was equally taken with Colin and the pair of us would regularly drive miles to watch him competing. Like any fan, the 1995 RAC will be forever etched into my memory, indelibly marked on my soul.

Having scored a press pass on the back of the promise of a few words for my local newspaper, Dad and I fitted the all-important sticker to the windscreen of his Vauxhall Calibra and then spent four days chasing Subaru number four up and down the country.

Towards the end of the second day, we noticed an enthusiastically driven Peugeot 307 was keeping up with us coming out of Grizedale. At a junction one of them jumped out and – in a broad Scottish accent – asked if they could tail us down to Chester. They were lost. We asked them where their hotel was and led them to the door.

They asked if they could tail us the next morning. We agreed and led them to Sweet Lamb. Decamping high above the bowl, we had our first chance at significant conversation with our newfound friends. Turned out they were mates with McRae. I was enchanted. Seriously. Mates. With McRae…

Having watched number four fly by, we were back in the car and off to the next stage. I couldn't believe our luck. We were now mates with mates of McRae.

My father was a little more circumspect. "David," he said, with a smile, "everybody is a mate of McRae this week."

A little deflated, I was back on the maps when I heard the noise. I knew we were on rally route, but I thought we were ahead of the leaders. Fortunately we weren't. I strained to see our man pulling out and passing the traffic. Approaching a junction, he was right behind the Peugeot. And then he was alongside with his door open. He was chatting to them.

I was in dreamland.

At the day's final service, our friends insisted we come over to Subaru's service area, where they had been promised hospitality. We followed. They were ushered into McRae's motorhome. We followed.

I was now beyond dreamland.

Feeling we'd intruded for long enough, I felt we should make or

excuses and leave. Having trousered a Tunnocks I would keep forever, my father struggled with the door to the motorhome.

"It opens out…" came the call from behind us.

So, with some force, Dad turned the handle and pushed at precisely the same moment Colin was coming up the steps to his motorhome. A moment later and we'd have flattened him.

It really was time to leave.

Next day, we were waiting for him at the end of Clocaenog East. And shook hands with the new world champion.

Four years later, nearly to the day, I was sitting alongside him in a Ford Focus WRC. A few words for my local newspaper had become the bottom rung of Motoring News' rallies department. Ford had phoned to see if anybody wanted a ride with Colin at its pre-Rally GB press day. I didn't say no.

It was mesmeric. Illogical. Inconceivable. And stunning. We were in Whinlatter, England's only genuine mountain forest. Known for its sheer-sided drops into the Lake District, there was plenty of belt-tightening humour as I settled myself alongside Colin.

Once there, I wanted to talk. But couldn't. Nothing I could say would be construed as remotely worthwhile conversation. I just sat and stared. My abiding memory is of a 45-degree left-hander which was approached on the limiter in top. McRae flicked the car and set us up for the apex so early, we must have travelled 100 metres completely sideways. For Colin it was a routine piece of showboating-to-order dialed up for a PR day. For me, a memory I'll never forget.Fortunately, I have plenty of memories of Colin. Unfortunately, you could never have enough.

Moving from national rallying to the WRC meant dealing with Colin on a very regular basis. To begin with, he was guarded and wary. But, the more time you spent with him (specifically time in the bar) the more you won his trust.

I was definitely getting there. His PR set-up a trip to go to Verbier for

the weekend. Colin was skiing in a 24-hour race and the theory was, it would make a nice piece.

My wife Sandra and I flew to Geneva. I'd warned Sandra that Colin could be quite protective of his downtime and we shouldn't expect too much. From the moment he saw us, he couldn't have been more welcoming. An afternoon beer soon after arrival turned into supper, turned into more beer, turned into green and red cocktails, turned into a proper weekend. I don't remember if he won the race. Beyond Colin asking a policeman if he really needed that hat, I don't remember much about that weekend.

Superstars are often celebrated for their ability to remain normal. For Colin, normal was natural. Undoubtedly, there was the odd millionaire moment, but the reality was that McRae was one of the boys. Proof of this came when he arrived in Autosport's apartment in Perth to be photographed by Colin McMaster for a feature. We'd been having… dunny trouble all week and when McRae asked where the bathroom was, we told him to be careful with the flusher.

He was gone for too long; the jokes were beginning the wear thin, when he emerged with a big grin. "Fixed it!" said the one-time plumber.

Bizarrely, once Colin had finished driving in 2003, my relationship with him really grew and I looked forward to the years ahead. Equally, it was that prospect of time aplenty which caused me to make one of the biggest mistakes of my life.

Mid-way through 2006, Colin called me to talk about his Escort Mk II. Towards the end of the call, he let me know he was doing a single-venue event, if I fancied co-driving for him? Of course I did. The downside was that I'd done four back-to-back weekends and had a family thing on that same weekend. I told Colin. "Nae bother, next time…" was the cheery reply.

Next time, of course, would never come. How could I have turned that down?

Well, I could. Of course I could. Colin was out of the car now; out of the championship. He was going to live forever.

And then came Saturday. A Saturday we'll never forget. The news so incomprehensible that it simply bounced off. It couldn't be Colin. *Couldn't* be Colin.

But it was. And Johnny. And two family friends.

Tragedy had struck on the most human level. Forget the sport, forget Colin's 25 world rally wins, his time as the champion of the world, forget all of that. A father and son had been lost. Two generations of a fantastic family, gone.

Around the world, all around the world, fans had their hearts torn apart that day. But the pain that I felt along with my brethren was nothing, absolutely nothing, compared with that felt by Alison, Hollie, Jim, Margaret, Alister and Stuart.

Since that horrible day, I've spent a little time with the family. And that time has given me a real insight as to how easily the word champion sits alongside the name McRae. This family has truly known triumph and disaster. And treated both impostors just the same.

The sadness eases with time. But then, every now and then, you catch a glimpse of Colin in a video or on the internet. There's the Lanark tone that became as recognisable as the bark of the flat-four boxer he used to step up to the top of the world.

And, make no mistake, he was on top of the world. His talent was as natural as they come; his speed ferocious and will to win more steely than any other. Colin saw opportunity beyond the limit, in a place where others dare not look.

The world is, by some considerable distance, a poorer place without Colin McRae and his pea in a pod, Johnny.

It's been an honour to join Colin McMaster in writing this book. I just hope, in some small way, we have been able to pay tribute to what was a God-given talent, a great, great guy, fabulous father and family man and an all-round hero in the truest sense of the word.

God bless you, Coco.

# Key people
## Those who knew Colin the best

The research for this book entailed lengthy interviews with several key people who featured prominently in the career of Colin McRae. They were willing to share their experiences, both positive and negative, of times spent close-up with Colin. These highly personal anecdotes and memoirs provide the main body of text for the following pages.

**Nicky Grist**
Co-driver to Colin McRae
1997 - 2002, 2005 and 2006

**David Richards CBE**
Prodrive Chairman
World Rally Champion co-driver 1981

**Malcolm Wilson OBE**
Ford WRC Team Director
M-Sport Managing Director
British Rally Champion 1994

**Derek Ringer**
Co-driver to Colin McRae
1987 - 1996 and 2003

**Robert Reid**
World Rally Champion co-driver 2001

**Christian Loriaux**
Prodrive Chief Engineer
1991 - 2001; Ford M-Sport
Technical Director 2001 - present

**David Lapworth**
Prodrive Technical Director

# 1968 – 1984
## Colin: the busy baby

by Margaret McRae

Colin Steele McRae was born on August 5, 1968. It was a Monday. He was born in the William Smellie Maternity Hospital in Lanark. And he was a much-wanted child – a first grandchild for my parents, however Jim's mum and dad already had two. It's from Jim's mum that Colin took the name Steele – it was her maiden name.

We were living in Blackwood, about five miles from Lanark, in those days. And it was to the house in Vere Road, Blackwood that we would have taken Colin home – if we hadn't still been renovating the cottage at the time. Instead, we went and stayed with my parents for two or three weeks while we finished the work on the house. This was actually quite a God-send as my dad wasn't feeling too well at the time and having a newborn baby in the house really took his mind off things. He spent all of his time, just focused on the baby.

Right from the off, Colin was a busy baby and, unfortunately for us, not a baby to whom sleep came easily or quickly. I think he stayed in our room for about seven weeks, before we knew the time had come for him to go into his own room. I don't think Colin really slept through the night completely for about two years. Alister, his younger brother, was something of a revelation by comparison and slept really quickly. It's fair to say, Colin wasn't an easy baby. He just didn't seem to need to sleep. Particularly not when there were so many more interesting things going on elsewhere…

And once Colin could walk, which he did pretty quickly, he wanted to go on adventures. He wanted to find out what was out there. As a toddler, to be quite honest, he was a nightmare. Jim's parents had a dog, a boxer. He was a real softie. One day, we were up at their house and Colin was outside with the dog. I heard somebody say: "What on earth's he doing with the dog?"

Turns out, Colin had found himself a steel welding rod and was trying to put it in the dog's ear. Asked why, his reason was simple: "To see if it would come out the other side."

Alister arrived when Colin was two years and three months and they bonded straightaway. Colin was never the kind of toddler to be jealous of the attention his brother would be getting, he just wanted to help. Or at least I think he wanted to help…

While Alister was still finding his feet, Colin had most definitely found his. There was an explorer in Colin just waiting to come out. At the bottom of our driveway, we had big double gates, which were tied in the middle, to stop Colin from escaping. Not long after Alister had arrived, I remember working away in the house and listening to the noises a mother always hears when young children are outside. I was suddenly aware the noise had stopped. I went out and found Colin's tricycle parked up against the gates. But no Colin. He'd used his trike to climb up and over the gates. He was away. The first place I looked was his cousin's house, where we would go quite often. He wasn't there. Then I saw him, over the road in a play park. I was so angry. But at the same time, I was so relieved.

He did the same again a little while later when we were around at a friend's house for lunch. All the children were called in, but no Colin. My parent's house was close by, so that was the first place I headed. And there he was, standing in the front garden of the house, crying his eyes out because they weren't in. I only wished I'd taken a

picture of him, standing there in the garden, in the middle of his big adventure with this huge pair of binoculars hanging around his neck. But at the time, I remember thinking: "What the heck do I do with this child?"

Cars were always Colin's thing. Always. Even when he was just two years old, Jim had gone away to pick up two aunts from Stirling and when he got home, Colin was straight onto his Dad's lap to steer the car into the garage. Aunt Belle talked about that for years! The car was a good place for Colin. He would sit for hours and hours in the car just pretending to steer and change gear. Obviously, the keys to the car were nowhere near!

When it came to school, Colin had nothing like the same enthusiasm; school didn't come on wheels, for a start! Colin never liked school. We didn't realise at the time, but he was suffering from Glue Ear, which is something easily put right these days, but it wasn't picked up so soon when he was young. He didn't hear things very well and, because of that, his pronunciation of words wasn't quite right. Potatoes were 'potatals' and windows 'windals'. I'm sure this had an impact on his schooling, but in short, Colin just didn't like subjects like maths and English. He liked technical drawing and woodwork, the kind of things he could apply some engineering to.

I could see exactly the same with Johnny. He was definitely a chip off the old block. He was always one for anything with wheels: two or four, it didn't matter. And he had the same opinion of school as his daddy when he first went! While Colin didn't enjoy school, he did make a lot of very good friends who stayed with him throughout his life. But, it's fair to say, when he walked out of that school gate aged 16, he was pretty delighted to do so.

◄ Colin showed an early aptitude for opposite lock.

Helmeted and ready for a big push on the trike.

Colin and younger brothers Alister and Stuart pose by Jimmy's first Escort.

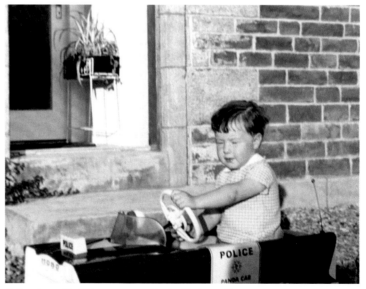

Colin enjoys a Scottish summer outside the Blackwood house.

# 1985 – 1986
## Two wheels become four…

by Jim McRae

When Colin finished at school, he started working with me. While he wasn't so keen on school, he had always been happy to work and had a Saturday job in a local garage for a few years before he finished school. But anything to do with cars, Colin was there.

I started rallying in 1973, the year before we moved to Lanark. And the year in which I started working for myself. I was chief surveyor for a big plumbing and heating company in Glasgow. And I was happy enough. But when a new boss arrived, I was quite keen to do something on my own. We were up in Lanark doing some work one day, when I heard about a small business for sale in the area. I telephoned about this on the Wednesday and by a week the following Friday we had borrowed some money from the bank and got everything sorted.

I had been doing some motocross around that time and when we got the business, I didn't really want to hurt myself and not be able to work, so I sold the bikes. At the same time, somebody I was working with got into rallying and asked me if I'd thought of having a go. I hadn't. But I thought I would. My father had certainly not been interested in motorsport beyond going to the odd race at Charterhall, so my interest didn't come from there – it was just something a bit more sensible than the bikes.

This wasn't a good time to start rallying, with the oil crisis going on, there were no events to do, but I bought an old Cortina. It cost me £300 and I worked on it for three months; the garage I built to work on the car at the house in Blackwood still stands today! I put a Lotus engine in the Cortina and I was ready for my first event: the Arbroath Stages. I remember the first stage I ever drove was up a kind of rough farm track and I came out of there thinking: "Oh, to hell with this rallying…" But the next stage was in the forests. I thought: "Ah, that's better!"

Jim McRae (right) relaxes on the 1983 RAC rally with co-drivers Ian Grindrod (left) and Gunter Wanger (centre).

Jim guided the Group B Metro 6R4 to eighth place on the 1986 RAC Rally.

1983 RAC Rally. 3rd place in an Opel Manta 400 was Jim's best ever result at World Championship level.

Like father, like son. Along a learning curve that would eventually lead to five British Rally titles, McRae Senior was also prone to the odd mishap. Here Jim's Vauxhall Firenza Magnum is retrieved from a ditch on the 1976 Circuit of Ireland rally.

I was 11th overall and first in class on that event. Three weeks later I did the Border Counties Rally and finished fifth overall. I then sold the car for twice what I had paid for it and bought the twin-cam Escort which gave me my first outright rally win, in my first season. I was definitely on a high about rallying after that.

After that, I started to drive Vauxhalls. I figured that using something a little bit different would get me a bit more recognition. It also got me some sponsorship from SMT, a group of Vauxhall dealers in Scotland and the north of England.

In 1977, I got paid for driving a rally car for the first time. Well, I say I got paid… it maybe didn't cost me as much to go rallying. The year after that, when I went into the Chevette, I think I was paid a bit more. And the fee definitely went up when I started beating Pentti Airikkala!

All through that period, when he wasn't at school, Colin would be at my side in the garage working on the car. He'd only go back in the house – and then it would be kicking and screaming – when his mum came out and told him it was bedtime.

As much as Colin loved cars, he couldn't wait to start competing – so he started out on bikes and was racing in the junior scrambles championships when he was 12 and 13. As well as competing, bikes were also the boys' first mode of transport on the road. They all had a 50cc bike as soon as they were allowed to ride them. Typically, 50cc wasn't enough, so they whipped that engine out and replaced it with a 100cc – but left the original stickers on the petrol tank. When they should have been struggling for 40mph, they were away at 65!

It's hard to say exactly when Colin drove a car for the first time. I guess it depends who you ask… Certainly, there were a few of the firm's Vauxhall HA vans which failed their MOT test and found their way down to the field at Robbie Head's house, where they would be driven around and around. When Colin reached 16, he said he wanted to go autotesting. I was actually quite surprised at that, I thought he might have stayed with the bikes for a bit longer; on the bikes it was all about speed and going as fast as possible, while autotesting was about handbraking a car around cones. But rallying was what he wanted to do most and this was the way to get into a car as soon as possible. In all honesty, I think Margaret and I were quite pleased when he left bikes alone and got into cars. But, we made it clear that if he wanted a car – it turned out to be a Mini – then he would have to sell the bikes and use the money he was earning to fix the car up. It was immediately clear that he had a real natural flair for cars. He was quick and controlled and won the 1985 West of Scotland Autotest Championship, with a 1275cc engine in the Mini.

At that time, Colin was going through what might loosely be called an apprenticeship with me. I'd say his time was divided equally between plumbing and working on cars. He probably picked up enough on the plumbing side to be a qualified plumber. When he got to around 18 or 19, basically once the Nova came on the scene, then we knew that Colin was done with the plumbing. And it was around then that he fully committed his time to motorsport, to building cars and basically getting everything in place to be out on the next event.

Colin McRae's began his competitive motorsport career on two wheels, riding in both junior scrambles and trials. Considerable success on bikes would help hone skills that would come into play later on four wheels.

Now fully restored, Colin's first ever rally car, the Talbot Avenger parked outside the original McRae family home in Blackwood. The garage Jim built to work on his first rally car can be seen on the right hand side in the background.

Driving a Mini with a 1275cc engine, Colin won the 1985 West of Scotland Autotest Championship.

Dressed to impress. Colin heads to the 1986 Snowman Rally in clothing that he would be paid handsomely to wear in five years time.

McRae

**1987-1990**

As Colin McRae's career progressed, there can be little doubt his surname helped open doors. But, aged 17 and with the ink barely dry on his driving licence, he was itching to get between the trees and compete – in a car he'd had to buy for himself. There were no top-down handouts from a five-time British Champion father. Throughout their lives, the McRae boys had to pay their way and that wasn't about to change once rallying arrived.

That said, Colin did borrow his first ever competition-ready rally car. Then again, Jim and Margaret were away on holiday and in no position to stop that assault on the Kames Stages in what turned out to be an ex-works Talbot Avenger. It was only later that the car's provenance was revealed. In September 1985, it was a tired club car with a broken gearbox. A new gearbox was the owner's only stipulation before handing the keys over. Colin and fellow Coltness Car Club member Barrie Lochhead changed the gearbox and prepared the car for the event. Colin finished an action-packed 14th in his only outing in the Avenger. Another Talbot – a Sunbeam this time – was found for the Galloway Hills and Crail Stages, the only other rallies Colin did that year. The Sunbeam – formerly the property of a certain George Donaldson (he of Toyota team management and now rally radio reporting fame) – and McRae Junior would be inseparable for the next season. Fortunately, it was pretty bombproof and a great way to start competing. The results were coming. People were noticing. But as trophies were gathered at a national level, it was clear that Colin's horizon's lay outside of the UK. And that meant a change of car.

The answer was a 1300cc Vauxhall Nova, homologated and ready to rally overseas. The Swedish Rally at the start of 1987 was a great place for a 19-year-old Colin to learn and Jim's co-driver Ian Grindrod would be the right man to keep him on the straight and narrow. Or that was plan, until a recce shunt left Grindrod nursing broken ribs. Mike Broad was a last-minute replacement. McRae made the finish of his first world championship event – via a couple of snowbanks – in 36th place. At home, the Nova rarely had time to go cold, competing most weekends, sometimes twice in a weekend.

"Colin was down in North Wales doing an event, the Skip Brown I think," recalls Jim. "That was on the Saturday. Anyway, near the end of the event, the engine blew, so a new motor had to be found that evening, which was done. The boys got in at about two in the morning from Wales, fitted the new engine and then headed off to the Bank of Scotland Rally event on Sunday."

And when it was on the road, it was rarely anywhere other than on the limit. As a consequence, it went through three bodyshells in a little over a season. And all three of those shells were fitted by Lochhead, one of the very original McRae crew. Spending so much time at the McRae's house, Jim eventually employed Barrie to tend to the vans for the family business. The vans pretty much looked after themselves. Barrie was around to keep the rally cars right.

"I had known the family for a long time," says Lochhead. "I remember going off to work and Colin would be hanging out of the window, asking me what I was up to – what was I working on? He was always mad for cars. And it was a very busy time once he started competing. The Nova came from Harry Hockly's place – I went down and picked it up. I think it always got to Harry that Colin was so quick in that car, Colin blew him into the weeds on his first event."

And he continued to blow the opposition into weeds, never more so than on the 1988 Scottish. More than a year into its time in the McRae stable, the Nova was beginning to look tired. "It was always safe," recalls Lochhead. "But we didn't really bother to make it look too pretty. We never bothered double-skinning things or anything like that, you always knew that it wouldn't be long before the next incident."

Jim was worried that 'incident' might come on the Scottish. Busy using a Group A Ford Sierra Cosworth to fight off the attentions of David Llewellin's Audi 200, McRae Senior still had time to spare a thought for a car coming a long way further down the field.

"As I was going through some of the rougher sections," he says, "I was thinking to myself: "That wee Nova's going to die there…" But it didn't."

It certainly didn't. Colin hammered the car along to move into the top 10.

"We were standing watching on the forest stage after Rest and be Thankful," says Lochhead. "And Colin came through having passed

Phil Collins' Sierra – Phil must have had a problem, but Colin was flying."

And he flew to the finish. A late overheating problem cost a couple of places, but ninth was still a massive result. And the second cause of significant McRae family celebrations. Jim had won his home international for the first time ever. Colin wouldn't wait nearly so long, writing his own name on the winner's trophy just three years later.

Through that 1988 season, Colin had been selected and won Peugeot's Young Lions programme (along with Warren Hunt and Iwan Roberts), which involved a series of national events in a Group N 309. The car was prepared in Lanark. And tested on the odd late-night dash to the shops.

"We were away to the chippy one night," says Alison McRae. "I was in the car with Colin, just going for a run after they'd been working on it, but the steering broke and we went into a wall."

That wasn't the only panel damage inflicted off event that year. The quickest Young Lion won a works-spec 205 GTi for the RAC Rally. Given that this was a different beast to the 309, Colin was given a test car just before the event.

"We were testing down at Beattock," says Lochhead, "and I'd just got in the car when we went off the road. The team weren't best pleased. I got some rollicking when I took the car back to them on a trailer…"

Clearly, Colin had outgrown the Nova. His pace in the McRae's unofficial test car – a beige, 1300cc Ford Capri – on the unofficial test road, a 600-yard stretch of rough gravel down the side of the golf course at Carnwath, demonstrated McRae's readiness for a bigger motor. Lochhead chuckles at the recollection of what was clearly a hard-worked Capri.

"A standard road car on knobblies," he smiles, "aye, that Capri saw some action. Luckily it had a vinyl roof which covered a few ripples…"

A handful of Scottish Championship outings in a Ford Sierra Cosworth were enough to lay the groundwork for Colin becoming the youngest ever Scottish Champion at the end of the season. That first big title would help in 1989. Jim remained a Ford driver, despite having flirted with a possible Toyota deal, and convinced Ford boss Peter Ashcroft to help Colin out in the British series. A Group N Sierra was loaned, but Colin simply couldn't get on with the standard car. The highlight of a season of cooked brakes and deep-set frustration was a class win on the Scottish. A factory Group A Cosworth was sourced for the 1989 RAC and the Audi Sport Rally, a month or so before was a good omen – Colin beat his father Jim into fourth place in the Welsh woods. But the RAC ended in the trees.

The following year started in the perfect fashion, with Colin's first ever British Open win on the Cartel International. An inch-perfect drive in an RED-run Sierra was delivered, despite Colin feeling below par himself. Despite that win, the season was already in doubt due to the lack of finances. McRae was third on the Circuit of Ireland, despite tearing a wheel off late in the event. He then rolled the car into ball in Pantperthog on the Welsh.

The car was re-shelled into a three-door car to take third on the Scottish, but every event brought huge pressure to finish. Failure to do so would seriously jeopardise the next event. By the end of the year, Colin would finally get his hands on a serious four-wheel drive rally car, in the shape of the Sierra Cosworth 4x4. RED ran him on the Audi Sport, where he was second and just a handful of seconds behind his team-mate Russell Brookes, and the RAC. The 1990 RAC Rally was a big event for Colin. Predictably, he bounced the car off the scenery, most notably in Cropton – after which the bolt from a farm gate was needed to secure Derek Ringer's door. But he was quick. And getting quicker. Fastest times came in the Scottish Borders and he was sixth by the finish.

His time had come. All he needed now was a break.
Step forward David Richards…

1989 Swedish Rally netted 15th place.

## Swedish Rally

February 13-14, 1987
Vauxhall Nova Sport
36th overall (Third in Class)

I got the phone call. It was Wednesday, February 11. I was at home and Jimmy McRae rang saying, "Are you doing anything this weekend Mike? Could you sit with Colin on the Swedish Rally in the Nova?"

Colin, with Ian Grindrod co-driving, had been doing the recce on the Sunday on a narrow, rutted stage near Hagfors. On a blind corner, at fairly slow speed, they met a local driving a Saab in the same ruts - but coming towards them. In the ensuing crunch Ian broke two ribs. They carried on for the next two days with the recce, with Ian hoping he would recover in time, but by Tuesday evening it was clear he wasn't going to make it.

I was about to do a WRC event with an 18-year-old driver. It was to be his first WRC rally, his first time on snow and ice with studded tyres, his first time using pace notes and his first time with me. In addition I had never done the Swedish Rally before. No pressure there then!

The first stage went very well. I immediately felt safe and was impressed with his car control. He was very quick and appeared to be listening to our notes. The times were good and we only went off the road once on the first day and that was on the spectator stage near Karlstad. There the snow banks were lined with spectators and on a fast lefthander Colin spotted his father and waved! He had seen Ari Vatanen doing that on TV many times and must have thought it was what top drivers did. In a flash we were in the bank. A few seconds were lost whilst we were pushed out. At the stage end I gave him a few choice words about concentration, not showing off and keeping his hands on the wheel at all times.

On the second day Colin's confidence was growing and he was now used to the grip levels of the studded tyres, the high speeds and the pace notes. There was a long undulating straight with a fast left and he clipped the snow bank and it dragged us in. We were buried in snow. It took us about 10 minutes to dig the car out but when we arrived at the stage finish they gave us a time only two minutes slower than fastest. I could not believe it. We finished 36th overall from 147 starters, a very impressive start to Colin's WRC career.

*Mike Broad, co-driver & broadcaster*

Barrie Lochhead, a neighbour, Robbie Head and Colin McRae in the McRae garage in Lanark where the little 1300cc Nova was re-shelled, more than once.

## » Memories of Colin

Colin asked me to co-drive for him on the Hackle Rally in 1987. We were in the Vauxhall Nova and I was no use to him at all. Watching him drive was like watching a concert pianist, even at that time. It was incredible, just all happening. We'd been lying around eighth overall in a 1300cc Nova and the times we were doing just shouldn't have been possible, but that was Colin. Then we got two punctures in Craigvinean and dropped back. I do remember the run over Drummond Hill – that was seriously scary. It was in there that I was telling Colin: "Steady, steady here Colin…"

The reply was: "Shut up!"

In the end, it was "F-ing shut up!" Colin's ability in a car was unbelievable. But it didn't always quite go to plan. For the following year's RAC, Colin was given a Peugeot 205, after a year in the 309. He was given a test car 205 to get used to before the event and we'd gone down to Beattock testing, when the car got wrecked. I do remember sitting next to Colin as he tried to fire it up and I said to him: "Colin, there's no point… that's the rear beam sitting up the road there."

*Barrie Lochhead*

Champagne in the hotel on the 1987 Manx. From left to right: Derek Ringer, Alec Campbell, Colin McRae and Barrie Lochhead gain an early taste of the spoils of success.

As Peugeot's most successful Young Lion in 1988, Colin was given a works specification 205 GTi for the RAC Rally that year.

Reasons for concern. The Nissan's speedo does indeed indicate a theoretical maximum speed of 200.

## » Memories of Colin

I loved being around Colin's house; there was always such a buzz about the place, always something going on. When we first started going out, I was always in the garage fiddling, if I didn't do that then I would never have seen him because he was so committed to the driving and getting the cars ready. In 1988, he asked me if I fancied co-driving for him. I said I would. The event was the Tweedies Daihatsu Stages and the car was a Nissan 240 RS. I had a quick look at the car before the event and it looked like a beast. Then I had a quick look inside and saw the speedo, which went up to 200. I thought: "Oh, my God! This thing is a space rocket! We're going to be going 200mph in the forests!" I didn't say anything to Colin, but I was worried sick. Anyway, the next day I asked Colin if we would be going 200mph. He said: "Alison, that's kilometres." I was like: "Oh right…"

I did co-drive a few events with Alister, but I wouldn't have done it for anybody else. In the Nissan, I was just a passenger, not really a co-driver. I wasn't scared though – I was in safe hands and we won! We did another event together in a red Peugeot and I took him the wrong way into the forest. We were first on the road and the arrows [indicating the rally route] had blown down; there were two roads up to the stage and I wasn't sure which one it was. So we took the second one and were away up there when we knew we were wrong. But when we turned to come back down, a logging machine had come up the road and the driver wouldn't back down to let us out. I felt terrible, but Colin was fine with me. He was mad with the lorry driver, though!

*Alison McRae*

Alison Hamilton, the future Mrs McRae, guided Colin to his first ever rally victory in a Nissan 240RS on the 1988 Tweedies Daihatsu Rally.
The picture shows him with Derek Ringer on his way to 2nd place on the Autofit Stages 1988.

▲ Colin McRae and Derek Ringer stop to change a puncture on the 1988 Manx National Rally.

◄ Des O'Dell with Peugeot's 1988 Young Lions, (left to right) Iwan Roberts, Warren Hunt and Colin McRae.

▼ At an early age, the unmistakable sideways style of Colin McRae was clearly evident, even in front-wheel drive machinery. Colin slides the Peugeot 309 GTi on a wet Skip Brown Rally in 1988.

Father Jim's concerns were genuine as Colin gave the wee 1300cc Nova a hammering on a dry and rough Scottish Rally in 1988.

▲ Father and son both wore Ford colours in 1989. Jim persuaded Ford boss Peter Ashcroft that the Blue Oval should support his oldest son.

◄ Happy days with Mum and Dad as Colin scored his first British Open Championship rally win on the 1990 Cartel Rally.

# Rally New Zealand

July 15-18, 1989
Ford Sierra Cosworth
Fifth

In 1989 we freighted two Group A Ford Sierra Cosworths down to
New Zealand for Colin and I to drive, with some support from Pirelli
and Shell. I remember on the recce, every time I saw a bad bit, I kept
thinking: "Hmm, I wonder if Colin will get through there…"

And then I caught myself out. I had quite a big crash in the dark.
We came up a hill and it looked like the road went straight on, but
it actually went left. The straight-on bit went into a lay-by. I braked
and chucked it sideways and tried to make the corner – if I'd braked
straight I would have gone into the lay-by and reversed out – but we
hit a tree and that spun me in the road, upside down and pulled the
back axle out. It was pitch black and all I could hear was [co-driver]
Rob [Arthur] moaning and groaning. I knew I had to slow the cars
down, but I couldn't find the torch. I could see something lying in the
road and thought it was a log… I went to move it, but it was a rear
[suspension] arm and I burned my hands!

Then Colin came up the hill. He slowed down when he saw us:
"That you?" he shouted, checking we were OK. Pulling away he
saw the car and stopped again. "Wow!" he shouted out the window,
"that's a cracker!" And that was it, he was away. I think he was
fastest in that stage.

*Jim McRae*

All smiles before the off in New Zealand 1989. In the end it was McRae Senior, not Junior, who racked up the repair bills down under.

Close to a roll, but Colin survived to go on and win the Yorkshire based Trackrod Rally in 1989 driving a Ford Sierra Cosworth.

The 1989 RAC was a rally to forget for Colin. An early accident merely a precursor to a rally-ending one, when he slid into fellow Ford driver Franco Cunico's Q8 Sierra in Kielder.

Colin survived ripping a wheel off his Ford Sierra Cosworth to take the final podium place on the 1990 Circuit of Ireland.

▲ Colin McRae and Robert Reid prepare for a windscreen wiper-less, flat-out descent of Drummond Hill, in Uncle Hugh Steele's Escort Mk II.

◄ No time to admire the stunning scenery on the way to third place on the 1990 Manx Rally.

## Hackle Rally
September 21, 1990
Ford Escort Mk II Pinto
First

I knew Colin McRae before I knew Richard Burns, I did a rally with Colin before I ever did a rally with Richard. The Hackle Rally in Perthshire was my local event and I remember being in a field [on our farm] lifting potatoes when I got a phone call from Colin. He simply said: "Fancy doing The Hackle at the weekend, Rab?"

And so we went off and did it in his Uncle Shugg's Mark II Escort Pinto. It was a horrible wet day, we won the event and I can remember there being about two inches of water in the bottom of the car. On the famous Drummond Hill stage there was a flat-out downhill bit and at this point McRae leant right across to my side of the car whilst I was trying to read the map (there were no pace notes allowed in those days). I wondered what the hell he was doing, then I realised he'd slackened off his belts to see out of my side of the car because at about 90mph the windscreen wiper on his side had lifted completely off the screen.

Colin was an absolute pleasure to be in the car with. He waited until you told him what to do, drove in a committed manner, somewhat flamboyant but never out of control. He was just naturally talented.

*Robert Reid*

The RED team worked non-stop to keep Colin McRae in the 1990 RAC Rally. Derek Ringer's door was held shut by a latch and bolt, 'borrowed' from a farm gate.

## RAC Rally
November 25-28, 1990
Ford Sierra Cosworth
Sixth

The rally started with the usual Sunday spectator stages and we trashed the car going through a stone gate in Chatsworth. We hobbled out to the stage end where our chase car crew called in a service van to change the rear suspension at a roadside repair. The next day was in Yorkshire, which basically went OK during the day, but in Cropton forest at night we really trashed the car! Again we got the car out of the stage and again the RED team made the repairs to get the car mechanically sound.

On Tuesday we went further north and after the first stage that morning, Hamsterley, it looked like we were out of the rally because the engine was basically gone; the head gasket had blown. The team had a spare engine in one of the vans but you were not allowed to change a complete engine so they decided to take the cylinder head off the spare engine. The mechanics managed to change our cylinder head but when we got to Keilder we were outside the maximum 30 minutes allowed for lateness. However, I managed to talk the marshals into giving us the 'correct' time, which was something you occasionally had to do as a co-driver.

We gradually moved our way up the field that day but as we were about to leave the service before the night stages, the starter motor failed. It would have been easy to have a spin in Kielder in the dark so there was no way we wanted to go into those stages without being able to start the car; this meant the starter motor had to be replaced. When we did finally leave the service we were running late again but we'd only driven two miles before a driveshaft broke so we had to go back to the service, which had just been all packed up, and get it changed. It was all happening; it was raining, it was dark, it was cold and the car kept breaking down.

At the overnight rest halt in Newcastle the team decided to do a precautionary gearbox change despite the fact there had been nothing wrong with the gearbox. On the way to the first stage the next morning, the new gearbox broke! Also the mechanics had managed to weld my damaged door closed and fitted a Perspex panel so that I could pass the time card to the marshals. The scrutineers said: 'No way!' and insisted that I must be able to get in and out without climbing over Colin, so the mechanics had to un-weld the door and fit a bolt and latch which they had got from a farmer's gate.

We had more mechanical drama on that rally than you would normally get in a year, however the car somehow held together and we finished sixth. Colin even set a couple of fastest times in the South of Scotland which really made people sit up and take notice. Ironically we won the Environmental Award, amazing considering the amount of damage we had done to the environment. For me this was a particularly memorable event, not for the overall result, but because of all the things we, and the team, had to deal with. We only had six mechanics in total and everybody worked really hard. That was the spirit of rallying back then. We were the first Ford home, in front of all the factory cars and this result certainly helped enhance Colin's reputation. Instead of being just Jim McRae's son, he suddenly stood out as being a really talented teenager.

*Derek Ringer*

McRae

1991

Yorkshire. Sunday February, 24. David Richards smiles his smile.

"I really believe," he says, "Colin is the new future of British rallying."

Little more than a month earlier, Richards had taken a punt on Colin. And a six-minute win on the Talkland Rally was the 22-year-old's first repayment.

Despite a headline-grabbing run to sixth on the 1990 RAC Rally (a performance which included four fastest times) in a Ford Sierra Cosworth 4x4, Colin was out of a drive at the end of the season. In part, this was a reflection on the British scene at the time. Competition in the British Rally Championship had been virtually non-existent for two years, while David Llewellin enjoyed a career purple patch and a sledgehammer Celica GT-4. The Welshman's job done, Toyota was out of there. For 1991, there was nothing, seemingly for anybody.

With typical vision and endeavor, Richards set up a Prodrive junior team with Rothmans backing. McRae and co-driver Derek Ringer were signed up for the British series, the RAC Rally and a good deal of WRC legwork.

The Legacy RS might not have had the same kind of grunt on offer from Russell Brookes' Sierra, but the Subaru handled beautifully. And Colin's bravery and boundless enthusiasm for carrying more speed than anybody through corners kept the Banbury-Lanark alliance out front.

After demolishing the opposition in Dalby and then on the Circuit of Ireland, Colin demolished his first Legacy shell in Wales on round three. He recovered from a Hafren roll only to finish the job a day later in Resolfen. The highlight of the season came at home in Scotland, when he didn't put a wheel wrong, won the event and shared the podium with his father Jim who was third in a Sierra.

Transmission failure on the Ulster gave McRae's title rival Brookes a glimmer of hope, especially going into the Manx – an event the Midlander had won three times previously. Prodrive drafted in French asphalt ace François Chatriot to try and keep Brookes off the top. In the end, Colin didn't need any help. A peerless performance led to a big win and one hand on the trophy.

The second hand was on the silverware a month later after a sensible drive to third on the Audi Sport Rally. After two years in Wales, the biggest prize in British rallying was back in Lanark, but this time with Colin, not Jim's name engraved on it.

Title won, all eyes were on the RAC Rally, where Colin and Derek would join titans of the sport Ari Vatanen and Markku Alén in the factory world championship squad.

Both Finns remember their first meeting with the young McRae. Vatanen's memory is of a mid-season test in Herefordshire.

"I knew the family, of course I did," says Ari, "and so when Jim's boy got in the car with me, I thought: "I have to show this young guy that the old guy still had a few tricks up his sleeve…" I think it was Colin's first time in the co-driver's seat. I came too fast into a corner and rolled. I'd wanted to scare him a bit to keep him in his place – but not that much!"

Alén was an immediate admirer of Colin's uncomplicated approach.

"He had no tactics," remembers Markku, "and just two possibilities: flat-out or nothing. And straight away, I could tell he was fast like hell."

Fast like hell he was and Colin led the RAC for the first time. He dropped back with a spin in Hafren, but was still firmly in contention when the rally turned to England's north-west. Unfortunately, he was caught out by a Grizedale right-hander which came quicker than expected after a crest. The Legacy rolled into a ditch and stayed there for 12 minutes. And then rolled again in Kielder, where it remained.

McRae's first season as a professional had delivered many more highs than lows. Beyond the British title, the highs included a wet TVR Tuscan race at Snetterton, which delivered an impressive eighth on his race debut, and victory at the Bettega Memorial Rallysprint in Bologna.

But, more than anything, Colin McRae had arrived as a force in rallying. The task now was to take the best in Britain to the world stage.

## Talkland Rally

February 22–23, 1991
Subaru Legacy RS
First

It was a very fortuitous set of circumstances that brought Colin and I together. Going back to the beginning, Prodrive's relationship with the McRaes started with Jimmy. Once I set up Prodrive, Jimmy came and drove for us on the British Rally Championship in a Metro 6R4. Colin had come along to many of the events, remaining quietly in the background. I followed his own rallying exploits, in particular that extraordinary 1990 RAC rally when his Ford Sierra was held together with baler twine. Some of his stage times were spectacular and he had made his mark. Everyone assumed that as Colin had driven a Ford in 1990 then he would naturally go straight into the Ford team to do the British Championship the following year. I met Jimmy in January and he was very despondent because, despite all the assurances, nothing was forthcoming (from Ford). Jimmy asked if there was anything Prodrive could do. I was not necessarily feeling charitable or being a visionary at the time, but I could clearly see that Colin had a lot of talent. So I took a decision to raise the money for Colin to do the British Championship in a Prodrive Subaru. I went cap-in-hand to Rothmans for sponsorship help as they had sponsored me way back in the 1970's and then had sponsored Jimmy in the 6R4. We did the British championship on a wing and a prayer, there was no spare cash at all and we were certainly not living the high life.

Colin was literally taken on by Prodrive as The Apprentice. When he was not driving in the British Championship he came in to Prodrive to help out in the workshop. When he was not doing that he would be driving a van and servicing on the world championship rallies with our other mechanics. He was to learn his trade from the ground up and on that set of rules that we based our relationship.

*David Richards*

Colin's arrival as a professional driver brought benefits…

There was nothing new in a McRae Circuit of Ireland win, Colin's first was 1991.

Colin's first significant Subaru shunt was on the 1991 Welsh.

## Welsh Rally

May 3–5, 1991
Subaru Legacy RS
Retired

I had learned early on with Colin's small offs, everything was understated. If Derek announced over the radio that they had had a puncture, this normally meant the corner was gone and they were flat-out on three wheels. In fact, we always attached the road tax disc to the roll cage, not the windscreen. The chances were, the windscreen would be a different one by the end of the event. This wasn't a pessimistic attitude, just good preparation.

*Alan McGuiness, Prodrive*

## Manx Rally

September 10–13, 1991
Subaru Legacy RS
First

In 1991, Colin became British Rally Champion. The interesting thing for me was that he really knuckled down in the workshop and got involved in all aspects of the team. In those early days he was the quiet shy boy from Lanark. His confidence only came out behind the steering wheel, where he demonstrated his exuberance. It was years later before his extrovert behaviour came to the fore. After winning the British Championship for Prodrive Colin clearly had aspirations to step up to the World Rally Championship.

*David Richards*

Colin and his future wife Alison celebrate early season success.

The first British title was delivered with a sensible third place on the Audi Sport Rally.

## Audi Sport Rally

October 19, 1991
Subaru Legacy RS
Third

Colin was clearly getting better and better and I wanted to give him a place in the Subaru World Championship team. This was a difficult time for me because we already had Markku Alén and Ari Vatanen. Ari is one of my closest friends but he was coming to the end of his career. I was faced with task of telling Ari that there was no place for him in the team next year and that, going forward, I was going to give Colin his drive. It was fairly hard for me to do that, but fortunately Ari understood the reasons. We are still friends to this day and the decision was proven correct.

*David Richards*

# RAC Rally

November 24–27, 1991
Subaru Legacy RS
Retired

This was the first rally where we used the Prodrive-prepared engine in the Subaru. It was born out of the frustrations of cultural differences between the engineers in Japan [Subaru Tecnica International, STI] and England [Prodrive]. The Japanese came into rallying thinking that you could take a production car and modify only what was necessary to allow it to become a rally car. Prodrive instead followed the rulebook, which stated which standard parts you had to keep on the car, everything else being free for us to change. The Japanese were very conservative and insisted that we had to prove that any standard component didn't work for rallying before they would allow us to change it. Back in those days Prodrive was not allowed to work on the engine and we had no access to the data or software. We decided to show Japan just what we could do with the engine, and the difference was night and day. I reckon that the best engine we ever had from Japan had about 280bhp, whereas the first Prodrive engine had about 320bhp. Mr Kuze [President of STI] allowed us to use the engine on the RAC and Colin was leading the rally before he rolled in Grizedale.

*David Lapworth*

Colin turned his domestic success international and led the 1991 RAC…

… until he rolled the Legacy, caught out by a right-hander after a Grizedale crest.

# McRae
## Rallying's first family

For more than three decades the name McRae featured on the results of World Rally Championship rounds as Jimmy, Colin and Alister racked up 246 starts at the highest level between them.

All three of Lanark's finest won the British Rally Championship title, with Colin and Alister winning the title three times in five years, between 1991 and 1995. But the boys never came close to the national success Jimmy enjoyed. McRae Senior remains Britain's most successful driver at home, taking what was then called the British Open Rally Championship five times in eight years.

Domestically, the family was never stronger than on the 1992 Scottish Rally, when Colin won the event in a Subaru Legacy RS, with Alister second overall but first in Group N in a Ford Sierra. Jimmy missed out on a McRae podium lock-out, finishing fourth by just four seconds.

Internationally, Alister has continued to demonstrate what the McRae name means, winning the 2011 FIA Asia-Pacific Rally Championship. But, on the world stage, undoubtedly the biggest result came on the 1995 RAC Rally. Colin won the event and became world champion, while Alister finished fourth as British champion.

Jimmy and Margaret McRae looked on with pride at their very own Scottish sporting dynasty.

Father, mentor and gravel noter. Jimmy always kept a close eye on the rally careers of both his sons.

Team McRae. Colin, Margaret, Jimmy and Alister McRae pose for a family photo at the 1992 Scottish Rally.

▲ **Left:** Ford Sierra Cosworth registration number D541 UVW was used by all three rallying McRaes. **Right:** Alister McRae, Mitsubishi Lancer WRC, Finland 2002.

◄ Jimmy McRae slides the big Opel Manta 400, 1983 RAC.

▼ In 1986 Jimmy campaigned a Prodrive-run Group B Metro 6R4 in the British Rally Championship.

McRae

**1992**

By the middle of the year, Colin McRae's outrageous ability was blindingly obvious to everybody in Britain. Striding towards a second British title with such confidence, McRae mischievously asked Prodrive to swap his Group A Legacy for a Group N version, in order to get involved in a fascinating showroom tussle between his brother Alister's Sierra and the Subaru of Richard Burns.

A second title was guaranteed when Colin won every round of the series. He was made to work for that 100 per cent record on the season-closing Elonex Rally, however, when Tommi Mäkinen turned up in Telford with a Nissan Sunny GTi-R. The Finn was out for a pre-RAC test, but the chance to put one over on McRae and Subaru certainly appealed on a horribly wet weekend in Wales. McRae took the win, but only by two seconds.

Exporting Colin's talents was something Subaru wasted no time in doing. He would start 1992 on the Arctic Rally, as a shakedown for the Swedish. Colin had already competed on the world championship's winter rally twice, but experience remains key in Karlstad and little was expected of Vatanen's very junior team-mate. But when Ari Vatanen put his Legacy off the road on the first stage, Colin was the team's sole representative. Competing for a factory team on a foreign round of the world championship brought plenty of pressure even before Vatanen's shunt. Colin responded to that pressure... by leading. And staying in contention throughout. He might have won had it not been for a blocked air intake and a puncture.

And, if that result wasn't enough to wake the world up, his competitive return to Nordic rallying would do the job. If experience is necessary in Sweden, it's vital in Finland. Between the two northern European outings, McRae set fastest times in Greece and suffered an engine failure in New Zealand.

But the 1,000 Lakes would go down in history as one of the most memorable rallies ever. It's not often that the driver in eighth place stands on the bonnet of his car and is hailed a hero. It's not often that Finns hail anybody from outside their national boundaries a hero, but in late August, the country took Colin on as one of their own.

McRae's chances of playing himself into the event gently were shattered when he rolled his Legacy at the pre-event test. Given that the car crossed the startline with rippled panels, Colin thought it might be worth shaking the trees to see what he could do. The few he didn't shake, he leveled. And delivered one of the most breathtaking drives in the history of the sport. He rolled twice more (the Subaru was reckoned to have been sumpguard up 13 times in total...) but demonstrated immense commitment, not to mention the strength of the Subaru.

Mid-year, Prodrive's BMW-based British Touring Car Championship programme gave McRae a chance to star on a racetrack. He didn't disappoint, taking eighth in the first Knockhill race. He was then excluded for nudging Matt Neal into a spin in a wet second race. Neal was furious. So was his father – who demanded to see McRae in order to remove his head from his shoulders. Fortunately, a quick-thinking team member said Colin had departed. Once Neal did depart, Colin emerged from the motorhome looking more than a little sheepish...

The end of the WRC season offered some major financial incentive for McRae; to mark the end of its sponsorship of the RAC Rally, Lombard was offering £100,000 to any British winner. As if the McRae story needed any more publicity...

Once again, Colin led through Wales, but Grizedale would be his undoing. A blind-brow meeting with a spectator forced the Subaru up a bank and damaged the suspension, then he got a puncture, then the brakes failed leading to a broken driveshaft.

Lombard's money was safe.

After leading the 1991 RAC Rally, McRae continued to demonstrate his WRC ability with a storming run to second on the Swedish a few months later.

## Swedish Rally

February 13–16, 1992
Subaru Legacy RS
Second

Some people think all drivers are tight with their money, but for me Colin was one of the most generous individuals I have ever known. In 1992 he nearly won the Swedish rally. At the big after rally party he put his credit card behind the bar. Everybody was drinking on his account. When I say everybody, it wasn't just Subaru people, it was everybody on that Swedish rally!

*Christian Loriaux*

The 1992 Scottish was the McRae family's finest hour in the British Rally Championship. Colin won, Alister was second and Jimmy was fourth.

## Scottish Rally

June 13–15, 1992
Subaru Legacy RS
First

Colin won the 1992 Scottish Rally despite experiencing engine problems throughout. On the last day, nursing his engine, Colin was running really late on the road. Richard Burns and I went off into a ditch and Colin actually stopped on the stage and offered to pull us out. He was leading the rally by about three minutes but we decided not to risk knackering his engine any more, so we declined his help.

This did show us that, while there was always a rivalry, there was always a friendship between Colin and Richard. Certainly, in the end, there was a huge mutual respect.

*Robert Reid*

◀ The calm before the storm... the front of the BMW bears the scars of contact with Matt Neal at a one-off Knockhill BTCC outing for McRae.

▼ Colin pictured before the Neal incident – he made himself scarce afterwards. Matt's Dad wasn't keen on lunch with David Richards...

# British Touring Car Championship Knockhill, Scotland

July 26, 1992
BMW 318is
Race 1: Eighth
Race 2: Disqualified

Prodrive ran BMW's racing team in the British Touring Car Championship and I promised Colin that he could have a race in one of these cars. The obvious thing to do was to take him to Scotland and let him have a crack at Knockhill. We thought he would be pretty quick, but you have to consider that the rest of the lads race these cars week-in week-out so there was no way he was ever going to be at the front of the grid. Nevertheless he acquitted himself really well, except in the second race he had a bit of an incident with Matt Neal. Matt's father Steve, who's a fairly large figure, came storming across the paddock after the race saying he was going to "knock Colin's block off." We had to somehow get Colin out of the circuit without him seeing Steve Neal, but he did get a small reprimand from the stewards. It all helped Colin continue on his route to national hero status, something he achieved in later life.

*David Richards*

British Touring Cars aren't the easiest things to drive and I think Colin struggled to get his head round them in the dry. It poured down with rain for the race and because the BMWs had anti-lock brakes he found the car came alive. Like all the BMW drivers, he was making progress through the field with the advantage of ABS. When he came up behind me, much to the amusement of the Scottish fans, he punted me off. Colin wouldn't talk to me about it afterwards so my dad went to speak to David Richards. He could see my dad was upset and said, "Steve, lets do lunch next week and we'll talk about it." To which dad replied: "Do lunch? I want to rip his head off and shit down his neck!" Which was unfortunate because it was broadcast on live television.

It was only afterwards we found out that Colin didn't have a race licence; he only had a rally licence. Because he had deliberately taken me out of the race, he was hauled up in front of the race stewards for punishment. He just sat there nonchalantly, safe in the knowledge that they couldn't do anything to him because he didn't have a race licence to endorse.

*Matt Neal, multiple BTCC Champion*

Corporate Colin. And what about those socks…

## » Memories of Colin

During the British Championship years I got to know Colin reasonably well and I think we developed some mutual respect. I realised that he had to have a certain amount of freedom and a long lead at times, yet there were times when we both knew that he needed a firm dictate. Jimmy was a great person for steering Colin in a certain way, but it is always difficult for a father to make the ultimate tough decisions. There were occasions when things went wrong for Colin and the red-mist came down, then we had to have some very tough words. It was also about survival for Prodrive, because we were getting to the point where we couldn't afford the accidents anymore. We were a small operation with modest budgets and I could turn the tap off at any time for Colin.

*David Richards*

## Rally Finland
August 27–30, 1992
Subaru Legacy RS
Eighth

Subaru were the new-kids-on-the-block in terms of teams. There was Lancia and Toyota who were super-organised and then we turned up in our gold trousers with pink jackets, putting on quite a show, without really knowing what we were doing. We weren't a big team back then and for us to run two cars in Finland we had to take everybody, including the lad out of the stores. In fact, if your wife could have inflated a tyre then she could have come too – it was all hands to the pump.

Colin had a massive crash on the pre-event test and we had to saw the front off the recce car to put on his rally car. In the rally itself he had two more big accidents. We worked out that, in the week he was in Finland, Colin rolled the car 13 times. It became a sort of challenge for the team; the irony being, the harder he hit the car, the more determined we were to keep him going.

Colin's absolute refusal to be beaten by Finland sealed his reputation and also helped the team gain a lot of respect as well. It has always stuck in the mind, as a bit of a turning point, where we thought as a team: "We're actually quite good at this."

*Nigel Riddle, Prodrive*

McRae made his mark on Finland (and its trees) in 1992. The record books reflect a rather mundane eighth; the team remembers a Legacy rolled 13 times.

Colin had been given the opportunity to compete in Finland as a reward for his British Championship wins. Little did we know what we were in for? We arranged a small shakedown test the day before scrutineering; this is when the poor Legacy got its first taste of what was to come. Colin rolled, damaging the car quite badly. Meaning the start would be touch and go. Any other team, any other driver, would have just gone home.

We got the car back to the workshop and stripped it down, almost back to a bare shell. Nigel Riddle arranged for a chassis jig to be sent from Helsinki, while other members of the team raided the recce car for parts to repair the rally car. This was not just a few bits – it was most of the front end, including a chassis leg. The work involved every member of the team, from David Richards down to the motorhome staff, working throughout the night because we had scrutineering at three o'clock the following afternoon. Of course, it was completed on time. Just. The paint was still soft; when the scrutineer sealed the turbo, he ended up with white paint all over his arm.

On the rally, the whole team got a terrific buzz every time we had to work to repair Colin's car. We became very good at fixing the car in the correct priority: safety first, performance second, looks third. Colin had a slightly different view. Yes, it had to be safe, but things like suspension, roll-bars, bodywork, perfect wheel alignment and even windscreens (Derek always carried goggles in his pace note bag) where just optional extras. The single most important thing to Colin was the steering wheel had to be straight. He could drive around any imperfections in the car, providing the wheel was straight. For him there was never any question the car would not be leaving the next service, he had 100 per cent confidence in the team; the last accident was history, he was already thinking about the next stage.

After the rally I collected that car from Parc Fermé. Remarkably, despite the external damage, it drove really well. The steering was still straight, the brakes were good and the engine felt fantastic.

*Alan McGuiness, Prodrive*

McRae

1993

CARO

1988–1984 1985–1986 1987–1990 1991 1992 1993 1994 1995 1996 1997 1998 1999 2000 2001 2002 2003 2004 2005 2006 2007

With a new three-year agreement signed, Colin departed the British rally championship for good, bound for an Asia-Pacific programme, with as much world championship action as economically possible.

Once again, the British media held its breath in Sweden as McRae led and looked comfortable. A broken driveshaft and an electrical fault turned first into third and it was a mark of Colin's increasing speed and confidence that the bottom step of the podium brought such disappointment for the Scot.

In his first season with the full team, there were plenty of lessons still to be learned. He and Derek would learn even more when they took on Africa in a 660cc Subaru city car named the Vivio. Astonishingly, he whipped the car into fourth place before the suspension predictably fell apart.

Having struggled on the asphalt stages in Portugal earlier in the season, McRae took a methodical approach to his Corsican debut. He learned plenty and came away with fifth.

Was it time for people to talk of a maturing McRae?

Maybe.

David Richards definitely thought otherwise after the Acropolis. Richards was jumping for joy as Vatanen and McRae went one-two through the opening day in Greece. A day later and he went through the roof. McRae had pushed to try and close the gap on his team-mate and ripped the suspension off the car on the pitiless roads close to Itea. A couple of hours later Vatanen's rally ended when, blinded by the sun, he put his Legacy in the trees on Tarzan. An accident which the Finn rates as one of his biggest regrets to this day.

McRae's punishment was a longer-than-planned stay in Asia. Once he completed Rally New Zealand, he would go to Malaysia for the APRC round, rather than returning north of the equator for Finland.

The bad boy turned good in Auckland. Very good, in fact.

As well as contesting the Legacy at the highest level, Prodrive had been busy readying its replacement: the Impreza 555. There was, however, a rather tricky impasse looming on the horizon. The Japanese wanted the Legacy to win before the new car was deployed; consigning the RS to history before a victory could be interpreted as failure for the project. Fortunately, McRae found form on just his third visit to the North Island and a spellbinding run through Motu was the platform for a historic win.

Ironically, Markku Alén stepped in for the 555's debut in Finland and crashed it a handful of corners in.

McRae meanwhile scored a predictable win in Malaysia before confronting genuine tragedy in Australia. Subaru driver Possum Bourne crashed off the road, his co-driver Rodger Freeth died from injuries sustained.

Colin waved goodbye to the Legacy with a pre-agreed second to Vatanen on the Hong Kong-Beijing before stepping aboard an Impreza competitively for the first time on the RAC Rally. For the third year in succession, he would lead his home round of the championship. And this year he led further into the RAC than before, only for a tree branch to pierce the car's radiator in Kershope. The flat-four was cooked. It was time for a new year.

## Rally of Portugal
March 3–6, 1993
Subaru Legacy RS
Seventh

In true David Richards style, he had secured the services
of rally legend Markku Alén to drive for Subaru in the World
Rally Championship. Colin's programme was the British Rally
Championship, however he often came out on WRC rallies, which
strengthened his relationship with the team, gave him the opportunity
to experience the events and learn from Markku. I remember we
were in Estoril, the night before the start of Rally of Portugal. Colin
innocently asked Markku if he knew a good place to go and set-up
the spot lamps on the rally car. Markku replied: "Arganil," which was
about 300 kilometres away. Typical Markku. Typical Colin!

*Alan McGuiness, Prodrive*

### » Memories of Colin

Colin and I always used to play practical jokes on one
another. I had bought a brand new carbon fibre briefcase and
I was rushing to the airport to catch a flight, really tight on
time. I tried to open my briefcase and of course, behind my
back, Colin had been in there and changed the combination
code. I didn't have the time to try out 1000 combination
numbers. I was going to miss my plane, so eventually I had to
break into this new briefcase. I got my phone out, rang Colin
and said to him, "Colin, you bastard! You know I will get you
back for this."

From then on I always reminded him that I would get him
back for the briefcase, but I would wait for a really good
moment. I kept waiting for the right opportunity but I never
did get him back properly, so he can rest in peace knowing
that he definitely got one over me there.

*Christian Loriaux*

# Safari Rally

April 8–12, 1993
Subaru Vivio 660cc
Retired

Safari was a magical event that everybody wanted to do. Mr Koseki, from Subaru in Japan, came up with a scheme to take three of Subaru's tiny little 660cc, supercharged, four wheel drive town cars (Vivio) to Safari. He asked Prodrive if Colin would drive one of them. Prodrive said "Yes" and off we went to Kenya, without any idea what we were letting ourselves in for.

We tried to do a recce in a Nissan pick up truck. Pretty quickly we concluded that we didn't know how to make proper pacenotes for Africa and that there was no way that either the Nissan or the Vivio were going to make it all the way round the whole route. In the end we actually just recced the first two days of this five-day event and borrowed the notes for the other three days from our team-mate, just in case we got that far.

Two days before the event started we tested the rally car on one of the smoothest gravel roads in Kenya, and after driving only 30 kilometres, the car promptly stopped. The sun was going down, I had a considerable amount of cash in my rally bag and all the locals had come out to see what this strange small car phenomenon was

all about. I was getting a bit nervous at the situation. Eventually four local guys pitched up in a knackered old car and we persuaded them to tow us out. They said they had no petrol, so I said that if they managed to tow us out to the main road I would fill their car up with petrol. We only managed to get about 300 yards before this tow car expired in a cloud of steam.

Once the rally started, we were up to fourth place after the first couple of sections, but there was no way this was going to last. Near the end of the fifth section the front suspension broke completely going into a river crossing. And then, getting out of the river crossing, the rear differential broke. Koseki's mechanics were not experienced rally mechanics, instead they had all won competitions to be the best mechanic in Subaru's Japanese dealer network, the prize being to go and work on the Safari rally. They had no idea what they were doing. Colin and I stood in bewilderment as they set to work on the Vivio and we were absolutely gobsmacked that they got us going again. This was great, so we kept going until the car properly expired two sections later, in the dark, somewhere near the coast at Mombasa. From there we headed to the hotel swimming pool for four days.

*Derek Ringer*

## Rally New Zealand
August 5–8, 1993
Subaru Legacy RS
First

One of the issues for Prodrive was that the Subaru Legacy was a transition car, as we always knew the Impreza was coming. The new Impreza was ready to roll but the Japanese were extremely reluctant to let us run the new car. They didn't want to see us retire the Legacy, which was a key model for them, without it having success. In absolutely extraordinary style Colin delivered us our first World Rally Championship win in New Zealand. It was an incredibly emotional event and one I will always remember. Prodrive was a small team from Banbury up against the big boys from Toyota, Ford and Lancia. To actually beat them, with a car from a Japanese manufacturer that nobody had ever heard of was something special. I enjoyed winning as a team principal far more than winning as a competitor.

After that New Zealand win there was a feeling that, in Colin, we had a sublime talent. If we worked with him and developed him, he could become something very special. So there was clearly a view from the outside that we were building a team around Colin.

*David Richards*

At 45 kilometres in length, the Motu stage represented about eight per cent of the whole rally, yet it was where 50 per cent of the competitors always had problems. On the second day we went into the Motu gorge in fifth place and came out in the lead. After that it was just a case of trying to control the rally from the front, not easy with the likes of François Delecour, Carlos Sainz, Didier Auriol and Juha Kankunen never more than 10 seconds behind. We had a big scare coming out of one stage when the oil pressure disappeared. It was downhill and we were able to roll down the road to our emergency service. Prodrive were able to fix it, the engine wasn't damaged and we got to the next stage on time. For the rest of the rally the whole team were on absolute tenterhooks and I think the only people who stayed calm were Colin and myself. I can't remember how much we ended up winning the rally by, but it was our first World Championship rally win.

*Derek Ringer*

Rally New Zealand brought the big breakthrough in 1993. Colin, Derek and the Legacy were unbeatable in the North Island.

## Rally Malaysia
August 21–23, 1993
Subaru Legacy RS
First

We enjoyed Malaysia; all the boys had a good time, mostly spent in the Hard Rock Café. The rally organisation, on the other hand, was shocking and a lot of the stages were held at night in horrible, slippery oil palm plantations. On the penultimate night we were leading comfortably when we went off the road at high speed into one of the many palm trees. The front of the car was completely destroyed but somehow Colin managed to get the car out of the stage and back to service. It was a real wreck; there was damage to the radiator, oil cooler, intercooler and the engine and gearbox had moved sideways in the car. The mechanics set to work in the dark and eventually they got the engine to run. The gear selector was jammed against the transmission tunnel and one mechanic smashed the tunnel with a sledgehammer to dislodge it. When he did free it, the car jumped into gear and ran over a couple of mechanics, fortunately not injuring them. There was still one stage to go that night but I had packed away the time card thinking that there was no way we could continue. Suddenly the team manager shouted: "OK you can go now." We set off for the last stage with six kilometres to drive in four minutes, otherwise we would have been outside the time limit. We made it and we ended up winning the rally in a car that looked a complete mess.

*Derek Ringer*

# Rally Australia

September 18–21, 1993
Subaru Legacy RS
Sixth

When the team initially heard about Possum Bourne's accident the news was that [co-driver] Rodger Freeth was out of the car and was talking. The feedback sounded reassuring. Rodger was airlifted to hospital, but we didn't know that medical complications began in the helicopter. It was close to the end of the day when we learned that Rodger had died in hospital.

It is always a difficult situation when something like this happens. We had team discussions about what was the right thing to do and we decided to continue in the rally. Rodger was a very popular member of the team and he and Colin were close friends. As much as it is a cliché, the team felt that continuing in the rally is what Rodger would have wanted.

*David Lapworth*

# Hong Kong-Beijing Rally

October 23–28, 1993
Subaru Legacy RS
Second

Immediately after Rally Australia we left for Hong Kong to do a low-speed convoy recce of the entire route, the plan being to return a few weeks later for the actual rally. Because of the tragedy in Australia, Possum Bourne did not join us on this recce, so it was just Ari Vatanen, his co-driver Bruno Bergland, Colin and myself. We left Hong Kong in pretty low spirits. The recce itself lasted nine days. The food was deplorable, the hotels were even worse, but it was truly memorable journey because of the incredible things we saw and how basic China was, politically and economically, at that time.

On the rally itself, the works Subarus faced no real competition, so, before the start, we decided in a meeting that Ari would win the rally. Ari didn't stick to the plan, however, when he crashed into a bridge parapet and lost a couple of minutes on the second stage. Colin was always going to let Ari win, but rather than simply slowing down, Colin played a five-day game of cat and mouse with Ari, making him drive really hard to catch up.

On the penultimate day in fog, we got to a particularly tricky stage, which Colin had recced with an enormous hangover after an all-night drinking session with [legendary rally television producer] Barrie Hinchcliffe. We knew the notes we had weren't very good, so we let Ari take a minute off us and that was the rally pretty much over.

When we arrived at the finish ceremony in Beijing's Tiananmen Square, Ari persuaded us that it would be OK for the three 555 Subarus to do donuts in celebration, so we did. We got an absolute rocketing from the organisers – it was only four years after the student protests of 1989. But, in our defence, Ari said: "What's the harm in leaving a little bit of rubber in a square, where the tracks left by tanks can still be seen?"

*Derek Ringer*

David Richards and Prodrive pulled off an amazing sponsorship deal with BAT (British American Tobacco), which allowed the team to move to the next level. But with that came the additional pressure to succeed and a massively increased schedule. BAT had significant interests in the Far East with its 555 brand, therefore in addition to the WRC, we were now competing in the Asia-Pacific championship with two cars. We all wanted to do rallies, even though most of us hadn't a clue where Indonesia was, let alone done a rally there.

In less than three months, we did rallies in New Zealand, Malaysia, Australia and China. It was tough being away from home for so long for everyone and in these situations drivers can really make a difference to the atmosphere within a team. Colin was definitely a work-hard, play-hard person. The harder we worked, the harder we played… If we happened to be on a 747 straight after the rally, it wouldn't stop the party.

Flying home after the Hong Kong-Beijing rally we sat upstairs in the bubble, Colin and Ari brought the trophy upstairs filled with champagne and the party started. We drank everything on board, then the crew went to bed and left us to it. Twelve hours later, we looked very second hand at Heathrow. But we had a great time – drivers and all!

*Alan McGuiness, Prodrive*

# Motu Gorge
## Rally New Zealand

Turn off State Highway 35, just east of Opotiki on New Zealand's North Island Pacific coast and you'll find a sign. "Narrow winding road next 48km. Extreme care."

Welcome to McRae town. The Motu Road.

Between the years of 1993 and 1995, Colin ruled 44 of those 48 kilometres, taking just over 37 minutes to weave, first a Subaru Legacy RS and then an Impreza 555 down a stage he made his own. The time might not seem all that impressive, offering an average of around 70kph, half that of some New Zealand stages. The time is impressive.

The Motu, you see, was a never-ending, sinuous series of second and possibly third-gear corners. A glimpse in Derek Ringer's pacenote book reveals the true extent of just how slow this stage was. The numbers in the notes – twos and threes – reflect the gear the car should be in. Fives and sixes were rare; the top half of the gearbox largely redundant.  Patience on this road was everything. And that's why McRae's dominance of it was so incongruous.

Don't forget, it was only 12 months since the Scot had been hurling his Legacy through Finland at an astonishing rate, rolling 13 times and finishing an entertaining eighth overall. Patient was not an adjective which sat easily in a description of McRae at the time.

But on the third stage of the second day of the 1993 Rally New Zealand, Colin went slowly to go very, very quickly. His fastest time on a stage he'd only ever seen competitively once before – in a Group A Sierra Cosworth – four years earlier stopped people in their tracks. But it elevated him from fifth to first and laid the groundwork for his first ever world championship win.

Predictably, McRae couldn't or wouldn't explain it. A magician rarely gives away his secrets.

There was nothing complicated about it, however. Colin just drove the car straighter, braked earlier – ensuring he was off the middle pedal at turn-in – and accelerated more progressively. The long lurid slides were saved for everywhere else; on the Motu, the tail stayed obediently in line for a little over half an hour.

A mark of Colin's ability was that he was able to use softer compound tyres than anybody else and still make them last. In 1995, Pirelli was rightly credited for mixing sticky and grippy boots for the stage, but it's worth remembering Colin had hammered all-comers two years previously in a less agile Legacy shod Michelins.

As the Scot himself observed with his inimitable waspish whit, the car was good, but he was better.

And, in that stage, he really was. In the depths of the forest which sits on the border of the Bay of Plenty and Gisborne regions, Colin found a new level. And frustrated the hell out of his rivals.

Only Didier Auriol, himself a master of technical stages, could really get close to Colin on the Motu and the Frenchman would cheerlessly accept at the start of the stage that he expected to drop half a minute to his Subaru rival. This kind of single-test dominance had rarely been seen in the WRC before.

As well shaping Colin's three successive Kiwi victories, a previously undiscovered imperturbability came out of the climb and descent of Motu. And it was the arrival of that new dimension to McRae which enabled him to shed the shackles of conception. And helped him to win a different way in Greece and Kenya.

Silver ferns, colourful skies and stunning landscapes are stereotypical features of the Land of the Long White Cloud.

This is page 33 from Derek Ringer's Motu pace note book, (stage 19) on the 1995 Rally New Zealand. As an indication of the just how slow and sinuous this road is, the first four lines of Ringer's words to Colin were: "30, two-left and two-right-plus, into three-left-minus tightens, 30 two-right-plus tightens-maybe, and two-left plus tightens, into two-right-minus, into two-right-line and three-left opens, into two-right-plus into two-left tightens-to-minus, and three-right and two-left-plus, 30."

McRae

1994

1968-1984 1985-1986 1987-1990 1991 1992 1993 **1994** 1995 1996 1997 1998 1999 2000 2001 2002 2003 2004 2005 2006 2007

For a year that ended with Colin dousing his Impreza in champagne and talking of titles, 1994 couldn't have started in more stark contrast. It was terrible. Worse, even.

There were two significant changes at Subaru for the start of this season, Carlos Sainz arrived in Banbury – as did Pirelli tyres, replacing the Michelins which had shod factory Subarus up to that point.

McRae's first attempt at the Monte went awry when he slid off the road on snow dumped by spectators. He made up 154 places after ditching the Subaru, but 10th place was hardly the perfect start. At least he'd competed in Portugal the previous season, which made his preparations slightly easier for round two.

Unfortunately, those preparations were derailed in spectacular fashion, when he and Derek Ringer suffered a monstrous testing shunt in the hills above Arganil. A tyre had rolled off a rim in the worst possible place, leaving the Scotsmen with nothing but fresh air between them and the floor 30 metres down the mountain.

When the rally arrived, retirement soon followed after the car caught fire. McRae did, however, manage four fastest times before the end came mid-way through the penultimate day.

Running second after two stages in Corsica, McRae would go no further after damaging the steering and knocking a wheel off his car in the third.

The next two rallies were arguably among the lowest points in Colin's career. After enduring the meanest and toughest terrain central Greece could throw at him and his Impreza, Colin fell foul off officialdom – and through no fault of his own. Having carried out routine under-bonnet checks of the Subaru, the scrutineers failed to secure the bonnet pins. When McRae drove out of the passage control, the bonnet flew up and smashed the screen. Subaru instructed him to drive to the start of the next stage, then refuse to leave the line until the team had been given the chance to fit a new screen. McRae did as he was told and was then excluded from an event which he held firmly in his grip.

Argentina followed, where a puncture on day one confined him to fifth place. A string of fastest times west of Villa Carlos Paz made for the perfect start to day two, only for a tightening corner to catch him out on the next one. A front wheel was ripped off and, to make matters worse, McRae refused to give in. He drove the car, inflicting mortal damage on the engine as the oil went south.

The team was furious and benched him for Finland, but he would go to New Zealand – the scene of his history-making first win in 1993.

McRae's mood when he arrived in Auckland couldn't have been more different from 12 months earlier. Having departed the City of Sails with a winning smile, he returned subdued. He was under cosh; his career hanging precariously. He needed a result, a sensible drive, a top-five was the target.

What came was a win. But not a swashbuckling, superhero-style win, McRae had driven within himself for much of the event.

And he'd delivered under the most extreme pressure.

He, Subaru and Scotland could breathe again.

McRae maintained that patient, precise performance through his first trip to Sanremo, where he collected fifth.

Then, when he came home, he let rip. McRae blitzed the RAC Rally to win by more than three minutes.

Now, the title talk could begin…

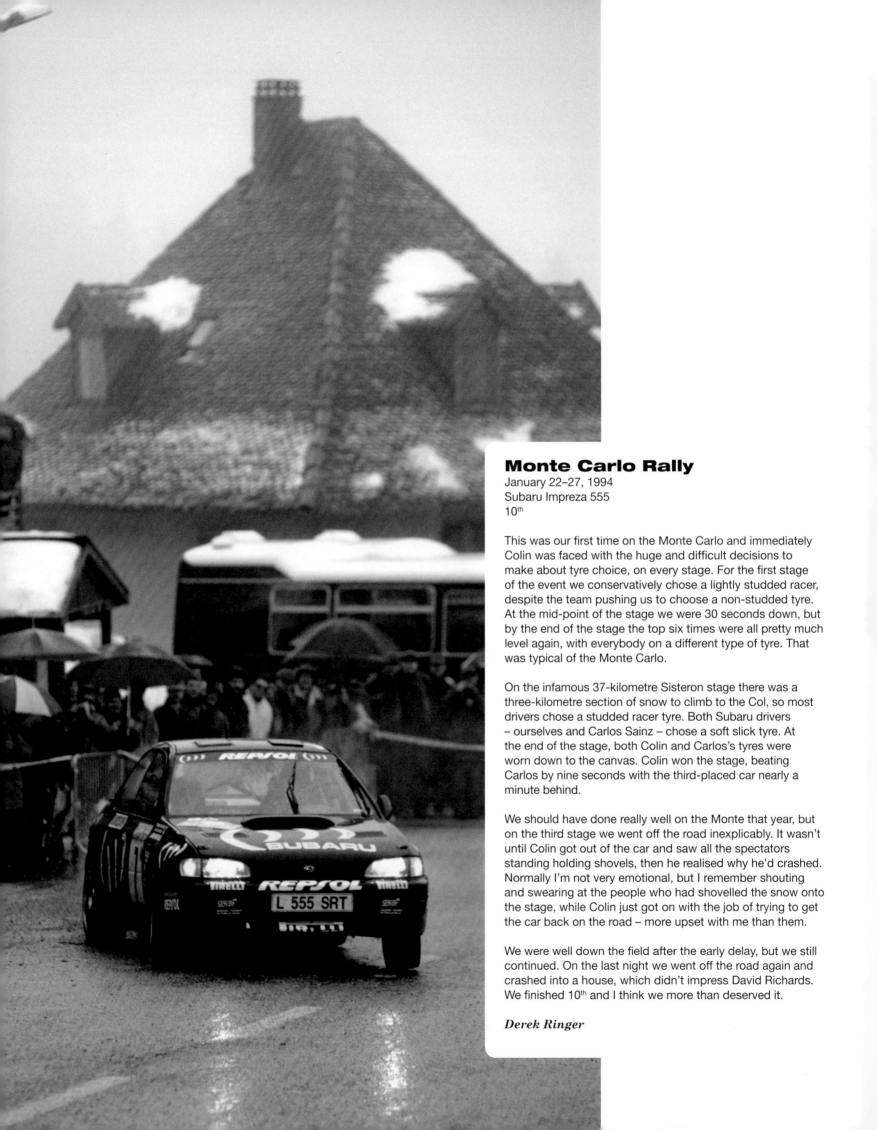

## Monte Carlo Rally

January 22–27, 1994
Subaru Impreza 555
10th

This was our first time on the Monte Carlo and immediately Colin was faced with the huge and difficult decisions to make about tyre choice, on every stage. For the first stage of the event we conservatively chose a lightly studded racer, despite the team pushing us to choose a non-studded tyre. At the mid-point of the stage we were 30 seconds down, but by the end of the stage the top six times were all pretty much level again, with everybody on a different type of tyre. That was typical of the Monte Carlo.

On the infamous 37-kilometre Sisteron stage there was a three-kilometre section of snow to climb to the Col, so most drivers chose a studded racer tyre. Both Subaru drivers – ourselves and Carlos Sainz – chose a soft slick tyre. At the end of the stage, both Colin and Carlos's tyres were worn down to the canvas. Colin won the stage, beating Carlos by nine seconds with the third-placed car nearly a minute behind.

We should have done really well on the Monte that year, but on the third stage we went off the road inexplicably. It wasn't until Colin got out of the car and saw all the spectators standing holding shovels, then he realised why he'd crashed. Normally I'm not very emotional, but I remember shouting and swearing at the people who had shovelled the snow onto the stage, while Colin just got on with the job of trying to get the car back on the road – more upset with me than them.

We were well down the field after the early delay, but we still continued. On the last night we went off the road again and crashed into a house, which didn't impress David Richards. We finished 10th and I think we more than deserved it.

*Derek Ringer*

After looking under the bonnet of McRae's Subaru in this remote regroup, scrutineers failed to replace the pins properly. The bonnet flew up, smashed the screen and ultimately caused the Scot to be excluded.

# Acropolis Rally
May 28 – June 1, 1994
Subaru Impreza 555
Excluded

In contrast to how it is today, 20 years ago it was preferable to run as the first car on the road in Greece, in order to avoid all the rocks that the rally cars pulled out onto the stages. On the second day of the event we were leading the rally, and we were exactly where we wanted to be: first car on the road. There was a lunchtime halt up in the mountains that day and throughout this time all the cars were placed into parc fermé. When we drove out of parc fermé to the start of the next stage the bonnet flew up and smashed the windscreen. The scrutineers had lifted the bonnet in parc fermé to check our turbocharger and hadn't latched it down properly after they'd finished. Colin couldn't see through the windscreen, so he decided to take the broken screen out completely, drive to the start of the stage and, under the circumstances, ask for permission to have it fixed there.

When I got to the time control I explained to the marshals what we intended to do, they didn't really understand what I was saying and they didn't put a start time on my time card. Our mechanics came to

the start and put in a new windscreen, while the other competitors lined up behind us. Twenty minutes later we started the stage as the first car and continued through to the night halt at the end of day two, still leading the rally.

Then the shit hit the fan. The organisers claimed that we had disrupted the rally and held the rally up, when in fact nobody had attempted to move us on and no other driver had attempted to start the stage. To make an example of us, the stewards decided to exclude us from the rally there and then, without any chance to continue under appeal. Colin felt really aggrieved by this because the whole incident was the fault of the scrutineers and we hadn't tried to do anything unsporting in any shape or form. That was never in Colin's nature - he was a fair sportsman.

*Derek Ringer*

### Tour de Corse

May 5–7, 1994
Subaru Impreza 555
Retired

During 1994 and 1995 Richard Burns and I actually did gravel notes for Colin quite a few times. Back in those days, at least once on every rally, we would all go out for dinner together because time allowed. Normally, after dinner, Richard and I would go to our rooms, while Colin would go out for a few drinks – but he was actually quite clever about it. If he was out on the piss with Luis Moya, Luis would end up in the worse state because Colin wasn't adverse to pouring his own drink behind a plant and then saying: "C'mon Luis, let's have another one!"

*Robert Reid*

# Rally Argentina

June 30 – July 2, 1994
Subaru Impreza 555
Retired

This was the first year we did Argentina, so we were all learning.
Colin had an accident, which pulled a wheel off, but, stupidly, he
kept going and going. If he had stopped it might have been possible
to strap the wheel back in place. But he didn't. He kept going until
he wore away the suspension. Then he wore away the sumpguard.
And then he wore away the sump. He only stopped when the engine
stopped, because it had no oil left in it. If a wheel comes off your car
there's no point in driving on – it's obvious. But for Colin, back then,
it would have been too inconvenient to walk to the end of the stage,
he'd prefer to carry on.

*David Lapworth*

A second New Zealand win in succession is celebrated with donuts and smoking rubber.

Derek Ringer with his baby child.

# Rally New Zealand

July 29–31, 1994
Subaru Impreza 555
First

My girlfriend Anne and her two sons came out to New Zealand for the rally. Our team hotel was near Auckland airport and we noticed a sign outside advertising a stretch limousine hire service. We spoke to the limo company, they let us rent it and they allowed Colin to drive it. Anne found an airline pilot and borrowed his uniform and cap, which Colin put on and then drove us around Auckland. We stopped at an ice cream parlour where Colin got out and opened the door for the two nine-year-old boys to get their ice cream. Colin played the chauffeur role brilliantly and he even stood next to the limo waiting for the boys to come back, they were absolutely made up by this. That was just typical of Colin, he loved to have fun and was great with kids.

*Derek Ringer*

I did the pre-event test in New Zealand with both Richard Burns and Colin McRae: three or four days with Colin and a couple with Richard. One of the days coincided and both drivers used the same piece of road. It was interesting that Colin set his fastest stage time on his second run, and watching him on one particular corner, I could see that he was about 10mm away from hitting the fence every single time. Richard was probably 100mm away from hitting the fence every time and he actually set a faster stage time than Colin, but it took him 10 runs to do it. At that stage in his career Richard was still learning his trade of being a world rally driver, a feature of which requires a driver to be able to look at a road just twice and then go flat-out on it. Colin was naturally very good at just going flat-out all the time and sometimes that serves you [well] and sometimes it doesn't.

*Robert Reid*

## Sanremo Rally
October 10–12, 1994
Subaru Impreza 555
Fifth

At Subaru, it was a big help for us when Carlos Sainz joined the team. Up to that point in his career Colin had driven an old Ford Sierra and then a Subaru Legacy – a car Markku Alén described as a taxi. Colin, basically, didn't know what a really good car was. Carlos came from the vastly experienced Toyota team and immediately told us that the Subaru Impreza was all over the place under braking, whereas a Toyota Celica would brake in a straight line. Colin would never have told us this was a problem, for him a rally car always slid around under braking – that's how it was. So, with Carlos, we developed a system whereby we locked-up the centre diff more under braking and this made the car slow down in a straight line. Having a guy like Carlos, with all his experience, was really good. He brought Subaru up a level, while Colin was always very good at finding the limit of everything. Those two drivers were a good combination to have.

*Christian Loriaux*

Back in the 1990s, the rallies were much longer and tougher. There were many challenges for Colin, none more so than his new team-mate: Sainz. The much more experienced Carlos thought the young whippersnapper would fall in line, but Colin was having none of it.

*David Richards*

# RAC Rally

November 20–23, 1994
Subaru Impreza 555
First

We had a great opportunity to win the championship with Subaru, a team which had, at that time, never won a title. To be honest, on the RAC, I felt they let me down completely. It felt like it was more important for Colin to win the RAC Rally that year. You know, it was a long time since a British driver had won this event and I never had the support from the team to tell me: "OK, don't worry we will support you. If Colin needs to help you, he will help you."

I remember when I went off the road, it was the final day and Luis was a little bit late [with the note]. We could have won and I was really not very happy about the whole rally, how everything went and it's sad that this happened.

*Carlos Sainz*

The old and the new… 1972 RAC Rally winners Roger Clark (left) and Tony Mason (right) celebrate another British win 22 years on.

McRae's RAC win launched him into Britain's sporting conscience and into the role of WRC title contender for the following year.

# **Colin** off-stage

Initially, Colin was not at all comfortable with press and PR – it was a side of the job he didn't like and he saw it as a chore. Ironically, in his later days he became very good at it, he came across as a natural person and very down-to-earth. Getting him there was a slow nurturing process.

I remember having a strategy meeting with a few of our guys to decide what we could do about Colin and PR. We knew it was like mixing oil and water; if we kept pushing him in a certain direction then we would alienate him. Whenever Colin met with the press he would just close up. He wasn't himself. So we took a view that we would avoid him doing interviews with the press and, instead, we would create a persona for him through photography and a series of stories fed to the press. We created this daredevil character and built Colin's image around that. It was carefully planned and we photographed him water-skiing, riding motorbikes and jumping off cliffs in Majorca.

*David Richards*

Colin was passionate about motorbikes, particularly fast ones. He rode race-specification superbikes at track days.

A Ferrari 355 GTS was one of several exotic cars owned by Colin.

Messing about on the water with fitness trainer Bernie Shrosbree in Finland 1998.

Always up for a bit of fun. Colin on his trials bike at his home in Jerviswood, 1999.

Popping a wheelie near Lanark, 1992.

Water-skiing in Corsica 1995.

Corsica 1995.

Skiing in Verbiers 2002.

Home gymnasium, Jerviswood 1999.

Jet-skiing in China 1997. Another organised PR photoshoot, all part of the daredevil character Prodrive wished to choreograph for their superstar driver.

McRae
1995

The hangover from Colin's first RAC win bit hard in January, 1995. He went off the road in the Alps for the second season in succession, hitting a patch of black ice when on slicks. This time there was no way back and his Monte was run on the second afternoon. McRae was back in Scotland when Sainz won.

Sweden offered little respite with engine failures all around for Subaru. The coating on the cylinder liners flaked off, clogging the oil pumps, with a resultant rally-ending increase in oil pressure. Much to his annoyance, McRae's motor was turned down in Portugal. Sainz won, McRae third.

No driver likes being given less power, but in 1995 that was more pronounced than ever. In an effort to contain the ever-increasing speed of modern-day Group A motors, the FIA slashed power by reducing the turbo's air intake from 38mm to 34mm. The cars were reckoned to be 50bhp down on the 1994 RAC specification. The Impreza's EJ20 engine didn't suffer as much as some of the others. Prodrive had been preparing for this moment for the last six months – fielding a course car for the previous season's Catalunya Rally (which wasn't a full WRC round) in 1995 spec.

Corsica marked the fourth round of a reduced eight-event schedule and the round-island classic was another nightmare as Subaru struggled to make their Italian rubber match the Michelin covers on the Toyotas and Fords. Colin's sixth became fifth when his team-mate Piero Liatti stepped aside for him.

Halfway through the year and Sainz led the championship convincingly on 50 points, while McRae languished in joint sixth, 30 points adrift.

Even the Scot's staunchest of fans couldn't really see this one being turned around in the second half…

The best news for Colin was that New Zealand would begin 1995, part two. And by now, the Scot's dominance of the beautifully cambered roads of Aotearoa was well documented – although it was in the painfully slow and twisty Motu gorge where he really made it count. Crucially, Subaru's plane bound for the southern hemisphere would be without Sainz. The series leader was at home in Spain, nursing ripped tendons in his shoulder after a mountain bike fall.

McRae seized the moment, won the rally and slashed the gap to 11 points in the title race.

Sainz would be back in time for the next round in Australia, but wouldn't see out the first day. A tree branch had pierced his

Impreza's intercooler in Wellington Dam, well south of Perth. Colin led the rally briefly in Bunnings but decided not to risk all in a flat-out chase of Kenneth Eriksson's Mitsubishi – the Swede finding blistering form down under.

McRae was up to second in the championship, and ahead of Sainz for the first time. Toyota's Juha Kankkunen was the only man ahead of Colin now. And he wouldn't be there for much longer…

While Kankkunen had never been completely at home on asphalt, he had always given good account of himself in Catalunya, but this was something else. The Celica GT-Fours of Kankkunen, Didier Auriol and Armin Schwarz blitzed the first two days of the rally, with the drivers blithely admitting they were enjoying more power from the engine. Post-event scrutiny found a significant irregularity with the car's turbo restrictor. They were excluded and would play no further part in 1995.

Before that sport-shaking controversy, there was the small matter of Catalunya to be decided. Sainz led after the penultimate stage of the penultimate day and that was enough for David Richards. The Sainz-McRae one-two was how the event would finish. In his defence, Sainz had never wanted this, but he didn't do much to calm the situation by making it clear that he would never settle for second before his home fans. Richards was adamant, Subaru's first title was at stake and nothing would derail that. Colin wasn't happy. He raced through the day's final stages around Vic to move back into the lead, ending the event ahead by nine seconds.

Sainz was unflinching. He had done his job. Now Richards had to do his. After a lengthy debate in the back of the truck, but mostly in view of the television cameras, tempers frayed, bins were kicked, but the deal done. It was that straightforward: a one minute-penalty in Spain or no car for the RAC. Classic rock and hard place. McRae took second.

The pair went to the RAC Rally equal on points. Subaru went as champions.

On reflection, Sainz now admits he didn't stand a chance in Chester. McRae rampaged his way through the woods, almost on a higher plane. He stopped to change a puncture in Pundershaw, won Kershope with the right-front wheel jammed in the arch and hit the front in Hafren. Sainz was powerless to stop him. Taking the Spaniard's words from the previous round, McRae was not about to finish second in front of his home crowd.

The rally, the title and the world were his.

# Monte Carlo Rally

January 21–26, 1995
Subaru Impreza 555
Retired

All I can remember of this rally was the notorious Sisteron stage, run at night. At the halfway point our notes said: "Patchy ice," when, in reality, it was full ice. We went careering off the road into the bushes in pitch-black darkness. As soon as the car stopped, I reached down to turn on the radio and call the team to let them know what had happened. I turned it on and we immediately heard David Richards transmitting a message: "Colin's off! Go back and give them a hand." To which Colin said to me: "Bloody hell, that was quick. David Richards must have direct communication with the Lord!"

It transpired that our team-mate Piero Liatti had already gone off on the same corner and had radioed in to say we'd crashed too. We helped Piero back on the road, but then he cleared off down the road without helping us out. We were out of the rally and had to wait in the freezing cold for about three hours until we got pulled out.

*Derek Ringer*

A tyre service on the Monte is a gamble every time.

Night stages have long been a feature of the Monte Carlo Rally as has guessing which damp patch has disappeared and which has turned to a potentially lethal patch of black ice...

Subaru dominated the bottom half of the points-paying positions in Corsica, with Sainz fourth and McRae (pictured) fifth after he and Liatti swapped places. The Italian was sixth.

# Tour de Corse

May 3–5, 1995
Subaru Impreza 555
Fifth

At the end of the rally we swapped fifth and sixth positions with our team-mate Piero Liatti, for an extra championship point. Piero wasn't going for the championship, he was an asphalt specialist and had been brought into the team specifically to try and take points off the Toyota and Ford drivers on the asphalt rallies. We gladly accepted the extra point under those circumstances, which were very different circumstances to the team orders that were to be imposed on us later in the year. In Catalunya there would be two drivers going head to head for first and second in the championship.

*Derek Ringer*

Colin's ability to pick up the spanners was well recognised by all of his teams.

## Rally New Zealand
July 27–30, 1995
Subaru Impreza 555
First

By 1995 I think every other driver expected Colin to take 30 seconds off him in the Motu stage, rather than Colin thinking he would actually do it. They were beaten before they started and Colin used this as a psychological advantage.

Colin learned, through the Motu, that if he adopted a different, conservative style at the appropriate time, he could gain a significant advantage. He didn't want to do it all the time, but he could sense the right places where he needed to curb his approach and this paid off for him in his later career when he won events like Safari and Acropolis.

*Derek Ringer*

# Rally Catalunya

October 23–25, 1995
Subaru Impreza 555
Second

We went to Spain with Carlos and Colin neck and neck on points in the drivers' championship. We got to the end of Saturday and Carlos led Colin by eight seconds, a small margin and it could be argued that their battle should have run its course – but Subaru needed to secure the title. Carlos was leading the rally, this was his home event and I was sure the pendulum would swing the other way two weeks later on Colin's home event. I had a chat to Colin and Jimmy outside our hotel and I was pretty confident that I had communicated that it was the end of the event as far as the team was concerned. We wanted both drivers to cruise through to the finish the next day and consolidate our position.

Unbeknown to me, Carlos had started to wind Colin up by saying that he didn't need any team orders to beat him and so, throughout the final morning, Colin started putting in some extremely quick times. Carlos carried on at his own pace and quietly Colin edged towards him and going into the last stage, was in front of him. So I sent the team manager and chief mechanic into the end of that stage to slow him down. Colin nearly ran them over when he went past. In my view he had clearly disobeyed team orders. I went to the finish in the high street of Lloret de Mar and had some heated discussions with Colin in front of thousands of rally fans. Jimmy joined in and eventually they agreed to check-in late (incurring a time penalty) and order was restored.

Carlos was convinced Colin was never going to obey team orders and it was a big surprise to him that he took that penalty. Of course on the next event Colin absolutely annihilated Carlos right from the word go.

*David Richards*

Driving towards the stages on the last day of the rally, Colin told me that instructions were issued the night before that Carlos was to win the rally. Colin didn't agree with these team orders and knew that if we did win, we would go into the final round with a 10-point advantage in the championship. There was a lot of politics involved in the decision; Carlos brought with him Repsol sponsorship money, we were in Spain and the team wanted to keep him happy. I'm sure that, in typical Prodrive fashion, they wanted to scheme things so that Colin and Carlos went head-to-head with equal points on the RAC.

The tension that day was immense. We talked about what to do and decided that, with Didier Auriol's Toyota only 30 seconds behind us, backing off was out of the equation. We kept pushing without making any mistakes and with one stage to go we were in front of Carlos by a few seconds, so the team told us that they were going to stop us in the last stage and hold us up so that Carlos would be back in front. Towards the end of the stage we saw John Spiller, Nigel Riddle and John Kennard standing in the road waving us down. I think Colin may have given a slight hesitation, but he just kept going straight on and they all jumped out of the way!

We finished the last stage and actually won the rally. If Carlos and Colin were going to swap places, it would have to be done with road penalties. The team weren't very happy, Colin wasn't at all happy and we were offered the choice of obeying the orders or not having a car for the RAC. I was the one holding the time card so I physically had to book us in late and I did so, very reluctantly. I'm sure that was the beginning of the end of my relationship with Prodrive. It's a company full of former co-drivers and every one of them is a better co-driver than me!

*Derek Ringer*

McRae's relationship with Sainz was tested to the limit in Spain.

McRae takes a moment to consider his actions in Catalunya.

I remember getting the message that we needed to slow Colin down. I was with John Kennard and John Spiller and we were told to go towards the end of the last stage, stand in the middle of the road and slow him right down.

"He'll understand," they said. I thought the plan was a bit ambitious and as I stood there waiting for the car, I was thinking: "There's no bloody way Colin would understand…"

I could hear the car coming well before it came storming into view. We were at the end of a long straight and there's no doubt in my mind that Colin saw us, but he kept going as fast as he possibly could, he had a point to make and it wasn't going to involve us three waving our arms. The two Johns had already dived to the side of the road, but I braved it out for a bit – until self-preservation took over and I knew there was no way he was stopping. I don't think he would have driven right over the top of me, but he wouldn't have batted an eyelid to brush me aside.

The following morning at the airport, the official at the passport control booth was obviously a bit of a motorsport fan and he recognised me from the TV footage. He got all his mates over to see the "hero" who tried to help Carlos the day before. I was famous for about half a day in Spain, on the strength of standing in the middle of a road.

*Nigel Riddle*

There is only one story about this rally. David Richards told Colin and me: "Whoever is arriving first the night before [the final day] will win the rally."

I arrived first.

Subaru made a press release saying the positions will stay like that and, for me, it's over. The next day we have no splits and we do the stage. Then Colin is going crazy. He took a few seconds in the first stage and then more in the next stage. I told David [Richards] that I could start to push again. But he said: "No, no, don't worry. It's clear we need to secure this result for Subaru…"

And then the story that is coming to the public is that Subaru is giving team orders stopping Colin from winning when he was in front of me. And this is not true. This is not fair. It was never like that. I did not ask for team orders, I told them I didn't want them. After two days, I was in front and I was confident [to win]. And then the whole story turned around and this was one of the most unfair situations. What is written about this rally many, many times now is not the truth. I'm sorry, but it's not.

*Carlos Sainz*

Rally Catalunya 1995

## RAC Rally
November 19–22, 1995
Subaru Impreza 555
First

As strange as this might sound, Colin and I didn't talk much about the RAC prior to the event, despite the huge media interest. We decided we would just go and get on with it, we both wanted to win - as simple as that. And that's what we did.

We had to stop in the Pundershaw stage to change a wheel, which is normally a pretty disastrous thing to have to do. We pulled up at a junction where some spectators were standing and I will be forever grateful for the help they gave us – they even had a trolley jack to help lift the car. That was just our luck and we had a belief and a feeling that, no matter what happened, it was going to work out.

I remember driving through the last couple of stages where the roads were lined with people waving Union Jacks and Saltires. It was a great feeling of relief to cross the line to win the championship on our home event and then we got a fantastic reception at the finish in Chester. To be totally honest, I don't think either Colin or I quite understood what it meant to reach that level and for Colin in particular, his whole world was about to change.

*Derek Ringer*

During the build-up to the 1995 RAC Rally, the atmosphere in the Prodrive workshop was strange. The car being prepared in the next bay was the one we needed to beat to win a world championship. All of a sudden it felt like Colin's crew were competing against Carlos's crew. This was a new, added pressure and it did cause a few strained situations.

Every service on that RAC was stressful, the only one who was not on edge was Colin McRae – he was supremely confident in his own ability and this really helped settle everyone down. Even when he ripped a wheel off and arrived at service on three wheels, Colin just said: "Ah, she'll be right, no problem."

The after-rally party seemed to go on until Christmas and the Prodrive Christmas party probably cost as much as the RAC Rally. The winning car was handed over to Colin as a present at the party and every member of staff got a book telling the story of 1995 season – each one was individually signed and numbered. As well as that we got an individually labelled bottle of champagne. I still have both to this day.

*Alan McGuiness, Prodrive*

Before we got to this rally, I talked to Colin and I told him that his behaviour in Catalunya was not right. I said to him: "Colin, you are a man and you behave, in Spain, like a child, not a man. And you are not like that, Colin. I know you. You like to fight and you like the straight fight."

Colin apologised to me for what happened. He was very strong on the RAC again that year. I couldn't beat him on the stages. I had no chance. But also after that rally I couldn't stay with the team, it was too difficult.

*Carlos Sainz*

We got to the end of the final stage and we were there waiting for them to come through. I was nervous then, really nervous. All the time I was looking at my watch thinking they should be coming. When they did come I kept looking at the watch again to see that they hadn't made a mistake and if Carlos was going to arrive really close behind them. But then once the minute was passed, it was just… yes! Once Colin went, Alister came in and took his best ever result on that event. It was a good rally and a good party after it.

*Jimmy McRae*

Even with significant front-right suspension damage McRae was quickest through Kershope. In his own words, not even a nuclear bomb could stop him winning that rally.

The trophy in his hands and the world at his feet. McRae celebrates with co-driver Ringer and team-mate Sainz at the end of the 1995 RAC. The party awaited…

We were all there in force. My sister and brother-in-law came down and we all went and spectated. We followed the rally around because obviously Alister was there and competing as well. It was good to have Jim with us, because it meant that we got in to places that we wouldn't have managed to find on our own. I'm not a good spectator, I've got more used to it, but I wouldn't say it was easy to watch the boys. When we got to the end of the final stage, there were so many people waiting to see Colin. It was great. After that there was a big rush to get back to Chester to see them at the finish. And then it was the party in a nightclub – Colin had his kilt on with some bovver boots, I was mortified!

*Margaret McRae*

Colin and I weren't together at the time. I was living in Canada in 1995 and knew very, very little about what was going on in the championship. I remember seeing something in the Calgary Herald about Colin winning the championship and I thought: "Hmm, maybe I'd better give him a phone…" so I called him to congratulate him.

*Alison McRae*

You need national heroes to get the British excited about rallying. Colin's character engendered great support in the UK, not just from Scotland, but England too and further afield. This was one of the heyday periods of rallying in Britain. I'd won the Word Rally Championship with Ari Vatanen 14 years earlier in Chester. I can remember that day well, yet the support Colin enjoyed in 1995 was just extraordinary. Rallying was getting the full back pages of the daily newspapers. Colin was world champion.

Straight after the podium we had a great party which went long into the night. Then it seemed to be party after party all the way to the end of the year. We went up to Lanark and Colin was given the freedom of the city. A couple of weeks later we had a big party for all our staff and sponsors, hosted by Noel Edmunds and his TV company. It was a fantastic evening with lots of silly games and right at the end we called Colin up on stage, pulled back the curtain and we gave him his RAC-winning car. I'd always promised him that I would do it if he won the championship, but I think he was starting to get a bit suspicious if he would ever get it.

*David Richards*

# Sainz and McRae
## Rivals

Carlos Sainz is an intriguing character. Carlos is more frightened of failing than he is of winning. On a number of occasions I've seen Carlos go to pieces when he has been leading an event. On the other hand when Carlos has been in second place I've seen him fight tooth and nail for the win. I think he feels that if he makes a mistake when he's leading then he feels he has lost the event, whereas if he makes a mistake when he is second it means he was challenging to win.

Carlos was totally professional, a real hard grafter who would spend hours and hours testing in order to do all the work he thought he needed to do. Colin, by contrast, would get in the car and drive it just as quickly as Carlos; he didn't mind what the set-up was. Dare I say it, but Colin's talent was such that it allowed for him to be a little bit lazy in the early days. But all that changed over time, when he realised you had to put the work in. Poor old Carlos would flog away doing all the testing work and Colin would come along, get in the car, drive it quicker and say: "Yep, that's fantastic." This was frustrating for Carlos.

*David Richards*

Citroën team-mates in 2003.

Subaru team-mates in 1995.

Sainz sprays the winner's champagne in Catalunya 1995, scene of McRae & Sainz's most bitter confrontation.

Crowds flocked to see the drama unfold in Catalunya, 1995. The partisan locals wanted a Sainz victory, David Richards' intervention with team-orders sent them home happy.

Friends reunited. Sainz and McRae both wore Ford colours in 2000.

Catalunya 1995, flashpoint.

McRae

1996

This wasn't how the title defence was supposed to go. This wasn't how anything was supposed to go.

It didn't take long for the realisation of Colin's dream at the end of 1995 to turn into a living nightmare mid-way through the following season. Undoubtedly, the pressure heaped on the 27-year-old was too much.

After walking on water for a day or two in Wales, he was now pretty much expected to tap-dance on it for the duration of a season. Surely, it was back-to-back championships all around, wasn't it?

Carlos Sainz, Colin's toughest adversary through his championship season, had departed Subaru and would be wielding an increasingly long in the tooth factory Ford Escort Cosworth through 1996.

McRae, it's fair to say, was a firm favourite when the season started in Sweden.

And that pressure got to him and it go to the team. The 1996 season was quite possibly the lowest ebb of Colin's professional career.

By his own admission, when he arrived in Australia towards the end of the year, he was struggling to drive. For years, he had been the very essence of freedom of expression inside a rally car; he'd made cars dance. Now he couldn't keep off their toes.

And the road to Australia was a shocker. After points in Sweden and Safari, Colin rolled out of the lead – and a near-certain win – in Indonesia. He made up for it with a beautiful victory in Greece, the foundations for which were set in the rally-opening Panagia test, west of Thiva. The number one Subaru stopped the clock 30 seconds faster than anybody else at the end of the 25-kilometre test.

Colin left Athens 13 points adrift of the championship lead. And with high hopes for Argentina.

McRae's second trip to South America started badly and got worse. He crashed a recce car and a motocross bike before the start, before breaking a rear crossmember three stages into the event. The part was fixed at service, but it took longer than the allotted service time, inviting a spirited run from axle stands to out control.

His rally was run one stage later when he rolled, but the ramifications of a racey run through service would be felt longer and louder. He was summoned to a specially convened World Motor Sport Council meeting in Paris and many felt him fortunate to emerge with his licence still in a pocket which had been lightened to the tune of $75,000.

The potentially worse news was that his time in the French capital coincided with the 1,000 Lakes recce. Colin crashed again in Finland.

Enough was enough. Something had to give and it was around that time that an ultimatum was thought to have been issued: change your co-driver or change your employer. Derek Ringer would be gone at the season's end.

And then came Australia – an event where Colin and the team were desperate for a result. Any result. Fourth would do for the driver who had won the non-championship event in Perth 12 months earlier.

Only seven of the season's nine rounds had passed but Tommi Mäkinen's breathtaking speed was enough for the Finn to clinch title number one Down Under.

Part of the double dream was over.

Ironically, on the eve of the end of the McRae-Ringer partnership which had ruled the world in 1995, the Scotsmen won the final two rounds of the championship to deliver back-to-back Subaru success.

Suddenly, they could see.

But what they could see was big change coming their way.

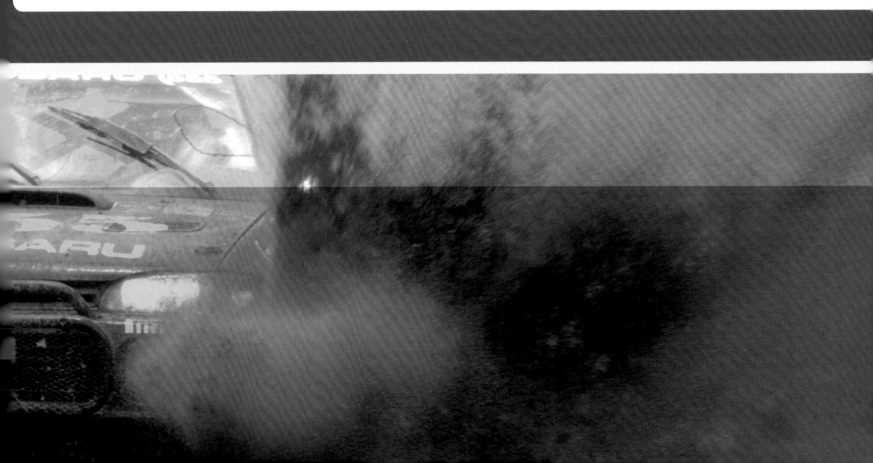

Starting in the snow. Calendar rotation meant McRae's title defence started in Sweden against Toyota, Mitsubishi and Ford. Third place beckoned for the champion.

## Swedish Rally

February 9–11, 1996
Subaru Impreza 555
Third

Colin got a bit pissed off that the studs kept falling out of his tyres. Because of that we spent a whole chunk of the summer going to dry tarmac test tracks, with our test driver ripping the studs out of snow tyres. The studs were glued in and we tested tyres with different types of glues by hammering round the tarmac and then counting the number of studs that had been ripped out. We made massive strides with the snow tyre development and the eventual outcome of working on that test programme with Pirelli was that we developed the moulded-in studded tyre.

*David Lapworth*

Summertime testing for the Swedish helped stud retention in the Pirellis.

## Rally of Thailand
March 3–5, 1996
Subaru Impreza 555
First

In those days the piss-up at the end of every rally was always quite big. After Colin won in Thailand, we had a huge party and everybody ended up in the hotel's swimming pool, quite late at night. Anyone hanging around in the hotel was thrown in the pool too, and there was beer everywhere. In the hotel reception there was a massive and beautifully carved wooden canoe, hanging up on the wall. Somebody shouted, "Let's get the canoe in the water," so a bunch of our mechanics lifted this big wooden thing off the wall and chucked it into the pool. Everybody was singing the theme tune to Hawaii Five-O. I took a bicycle and jumped that into the pool. Then David Richards came along, saw what was going on and said to the team manager, John Spiller: "John… I think I've just seen a bicycle going in the swimming pool."

*Christian Loriaux*

# Safari Rally

April 5–7, 1996
Subaru Impreza 555
Fourth

Mitsubishi well and truly outsmarted Subaru in Kenya that year. Things could have gone a lot better for us though, if only we hadn't have lost our helicopter! We had a puncture and radioed our spotter helicopter for assistance, the reply being: "OK, we'll fly-on and land. You stop beside us." The problem was there was a junction in the route where the stage turned right, however the helicopter missed it and followed the road straight on. We never saw the helicopter and ended up driving on and on until the suspension was destroyed.

*Derek Ringer*

▼ Africa's rainy season had well and truly arrived in time for the Safari recce – astonishingly, McRae's Subaru emerged from this Kenyan river without problem.

▲ Colin turns the bonnet to a bed mid-way through the 1996 Safari.

A big patch of mud allied to a committed approach wrote this Impreza off in Indonesia.

## Rally of Indonesia
May 10–12, 1996
Subaru Impreza 555
Retired

This was the first year for Indonesia to be included in the World Rally Championship and the stages were really tricky. We had been there in 1995, so we knew our way around, unlike all the other top drivers such as Didier, Carlos and Juha. Because of the nature of the roads, everybody else ran into problems early on and we found ourselves leading the rally by over three minutes, with less than a third of it completed. I remember saying: "OK, Colin, we can relax a bit, keep out of trouble and that'll be 20 points." To which Colin said: "Where's the fun in that!?"

Later on we had an intercom failure, so we switched to the spare intercom, which kept cutting in and out, probably due to the high humidity. I resorted to hand signals to indicate to Colin the severity of the approaching corners and, given the situation, we were driving much too quickly. We hit a big patch of mud at high speed, went off and totally destroyed the car. It was one of those completely unnecessary ones that makes you look like a complete prat.

*Derek Ringer*

Not even a late propshaft failure could stop McRae winning in Greece.

## Acropolis Rally
June 2–4, 1996
Subaru Impreza 555
First

Colin drove brilliantly on the first stage of the rally and we took 20 seconds out of everybody else. People seemed to sit back, scratching their heads wondering how we could do that, but Colin had just decided he was going to dominate in Greece, right from the start. Everything was going well until the propshaft failed on the penultimate stage of the rally. Luckily for us, the organisers had built in an extra 10-minute service before the last stage, anticipating that everyone would need new tyres because the stages were so rough. We sped through the service area, the mechanics fixed the propshaft and we just made it out with two or three seconds to spare before we would have incurred penalties and potentially lost the rally. I think that speeding in the service park did upset the powers-that-be and that was to have a knock-on effect in Argentina later in the year.

*Derek Ringer*

Martin Brundle gives McRae some tips on hustling a Jordan 196 around Silverstone.

A briefly bearded McRae proposed to Alison in 1996. She said yes.

## Colin and Alison

In 1996, Colin took time out to visit his childhood sweetheart Alison Hamilton, who was then resident in Calgary, Canada. The couple rekindled their relationship, which had begun in 1987, this time for good. Colin proposed marriage to Alison; she sold up her Canadian hairdressing salon business and returned home to Lanark. A wedding in 1997 was planned.

## Jordan F1 drive

In 1996, Colin achieved a personal ambition when he got the chance to drive a modern Formula 1 car at Silverstone racing circuit. The reigning WRC champion put on quite a show, which included drifting the Jordan 196 around the double left-handers of Luffield and fish-tailing his way onto the main start/finish straight, on full power. F1 Team principal Eddie Jordan commented: "Colin was instantly quick. Had he chosen to take up motor racing instead of rallying, I'm quite certain he would have been a Grand Prix world champion."

◄ McRae clipped a spectator early on in Argentina, their jacket is still attached to the front-left of the Impreza 555. The South American event was a shocker from beginning to its premature end.

▼ A PR stunt reduced McRae to a single horse power in Cordoba.

## Rally Argentina
July 4–6, 1996
Subaru Impreza 555
Retired

Colin wasn't really himself in Argentina, he had some personal issues and the pressures of the season were starting to get to him. There were a whole load of little issues adding up and I remember falling out with the team over a PR stunt, which I flatly refused to do. The day before the rally started they wanted the drivers and co-drivers photographed riding horses at a ranch, four of us had never even sat on a horse before. Colin had ridden a horse before and, if you knew what he was like, then he was sure to go off charging around on it. I thought this was a stupid idea.

On the first morning of the rally we were due to leave the hotel at 0700. Colin appeared at exactly 0700 and asked if there was time for breakfast, to which I had to tell him there wasn't. Colin always liked a breakfast in the morning so he wasn't best pleased. Next up, [technical director] David Lapworth told him there was a problem with his car and the team changed the specification overnight, not what a professional driver of Colin's calibre wants to hear. Then, when it was time to choose the tyres, we found out that Pirelli had been unable to get in to look at the stages so we had no tyre information to go on. So, it was one bad thing after another.

The first stage was lined with thousands of spectators standing dangerously close to the stage and, unfortunately, we clipped one of them. We got to the end of the stage and tried to tell the marshals what had happened, but they only spoke Spanish. Then the in-car radio stopped working so we couldn't communicate with the team, or get any stage times. On the next stage I read a pace note wrong and thought we'd just got away with it, until, two corners later, Colin hit something hard while shouting at me.

I have no idea what happened at the service park because I was at the time control and I didn't see anything. I don't know how fast Colin was going and he never even told me he had hit somebody, all he said to me was: "That was a complete fuck up."

On stage six we rolled out of the rally.

*Derek Ringer*

FEDERATION INTERNATIONALE DE L' AUTOMOBILE

**PRESS INFORMATION**

**WORLD MOTOR SPORT COUNCIL MEETING – 20 AUGUST 1996**

**FIA WORLD RALLY CHAMPIONSHIP - HEARING OF THE DRIVER COLIN McRAE**

The FIA World Motor Sport Council met today in Paris for an extraordinary meeting to examine the report of the FIA Observer at the 1996 Argentina Rally, relating to an incident involving driver Colin McRae at the Taninga service area of the first leg.

After hearing the defence of Colin McRae, the World Motor Sport Council recognised a number of mitigating circumstances, including his expression of regret that he drove at an excessive speed in the service area.

Due to the exceptional circumstances of this case, the World Motor Sport Council imposed a fine of 250 000 US$ of which 175 000 US$ is suspended, provided Colin McRae is involved in no similar incident for the rest of the season.

The World Motor Sport Council made it clear that in future infringements of this kind will usually result in the suspension of the competitor's licence.

Paris, 20 August 1996

**FOR MEDIA INFORMATION PURPOSES - NO REGULATORY VALUE**
For further information on the FIA, please consult our Internet site:
**www.fia.com**

8 Place de la Concorde
75008 Paris – France
Tel: + 33 1 43 12 58 15 – Fax: + 33 1 43 12 58 19
(External Relations)

After Colin retired from the event he and Alister went out for dinner, then disappeared off somewhere and no one could find them. I wasn't in Argentina, however the stewards got hold of me in England and asked me to track Colin down. Eventually I did and I told him to go and have a chat with the stewards and apologise to them. Then the slightly petulant side of Colin came out when he said he wouldn't; in his eyes, he'd done nothing wrong. When the stewards' event report came out, Colin found himself in front of the World Motor Sport Council for a disciplinary hearing. [Then FIA president] Max Mosely thought that, as a champion, Colin should be an ambassador for the sport and Max was out to make an example of him. Max had seen all the photos of Colin's daredevil antics and really believed that was his true persona. There was talk of his licence being taken away for a couple of events. It was [then FFSA president] Jean-Marie Balestre who came to Colin's defence. Balestre sat directly opposite me and spent most of the meeting muttering under his breath in French. I couldn't quite understand what he was thinking, but I thought he was going to cause us problems. When he eventually did speak he said: "Look, this is a young rally driver. What do you expect young rally drivers to do? They drive quickly. He is an exciting guy, why do you want to punish him?"

Ultimately they decided just to give him a fine.

*David Richards*

## Rally Australia
September 13-16, 1996
Subaru Impreza 555
Fourth

Torrential rains in Western Australia made the Bunnings river crossing much deeper than normal. Carlos Sainz became the first victim of the flood when his Ford Escort came to a spluttering halt immediately after the water. Luis Moya waded back across to warn the following crews of the impending danger. Despite the efforts of Luis to wave Colin down, the Scot entered the river at normal speed only to come to a grinding halt when the Subaru's intakes ingested too much water. First on the scene to help rescue Colin was a watching Jimmy McRae. The next three cars to arrive all had similar problems and got stuck, prompting the organisers to stop the stage.

Following the final round of the season in Catalunya, McRae poses by his car for 1997. The new Subaru Impreza WRC pictured, co-driver Derek Ringer not so…

## Sanremo Rally

October 13–16, 1996
Subaru Impreza 555
First

The whole year felt like a set of dominoes tumbling over for me, but they had been set in motion before 1996. There were a lot of politics involved and I will never know exactly what happened. David Richards wouldn't know what happened; Jimmy McRae wouldn't know what happened, everybody was coming from a different direction and they all had their own agenda. Nobody from Prodrive's management ever took Colin and me to one side to try and sort things out, instead it all just got out of hand. Between the Australia and Sanremo rallies I was told that I was no longer required to be Colin's co-driver, but I elected to fulfil my contract to the end of the season. So Sanremo and Catalunya became the two most difficult rallies I've ever done because of the atmosphere in the car, but we managed to win them both. Before Sanremo, Prodrive announced to the media who my replacement would be and I remember sitting on the starting ramp thinking: "There's no going back now."

*Derek Ringer*

McRae

**1997**

McRae
Grist

The championship that never came.

In a season of great change for the sport, the seeds were sewn for McRae making the biggest change in his own career. He won five from 14 rallies, finished second in the championship by a point and was clearly the quickest and most capable driver out there.

This was the year of the World Rally Car – a significant regulation change aimed at breaking down the barriers of entry to potential new manufacturers. The new rules meant an overhaul of the Impreza 555, which morphed into the Impreza WRC 97. Beneath the bonnet, the intercooler was moved to a much more efficient position at the front of the car (instead of on top of the engine) and the turbo was shifted, bringing alterations to the exhaust manifolds. There was more power, but not dramatically so.

The drama was all outside. The car was given, in aero terms, the bells and whistles. There was no doubting which team delivered the most attractive car to the Monaco start of the season.

There might have been a new car in Monte, but McRae's season started with familiar frustration in the Principality. A misting windscreen allied to differential trouble gave Colin and his new co-driver Nicky Grist little to smile about. They went off the road briefly in Burzet and again in St Jean en Royans, where they stayed.

Points were put on the board with fourth in Sweden, while the first win of the year came on the Safari – the third round of the series undoubtedly providing a 1997 highlight. For a driver whose reputation was based around a flat-out approach, the rigors of Africa were expected to expose this apparent one-trick pony. As it transpired, McRae had plenty of tricks up his sleeve. He won the event, heading Richard Burns in Britain's first WRC one-two of the modern era, but it hadn't been quite as simple as it looked. Final day alternator failure kept the Banbury boys on their toes and tenterhooks until the finish.

That Safari win left Subaru on cloud nine – it had won the first three rounds in 1997 (Piero Liatti on the Monte and Kenneth Eriksson in Sweden) – and McRae's mood brightened as he left Kenya with a single-point advantage in the drivers' standings.

Further evidence of McRae's evolution as a driver came with his maiden Tour de Corse win on only his second start on the notoriously tricky French island. And what a win. He went into the final stage seven seconds behind Carlos Sainz's Ford and came out eight up. Through the event, however, Colin had been forced to nurse his Pirelli tyres and not let the irritation of Peugeot's sensationally quick 306 Maxi get under his skin. Rain on the final leg ended the non-championship French flyers' chances and gave the Italian boots on the Subaru just enough life.

Those two wins aside, trouble was brewing. As part of the revamp of the Impreza, Prodrive had also introduced a wider track, aimed at improving grip, stability and weight transfer. McRae felt it made the car more prone to understeer and this spec change put him at odds with the team almost from the start. By mid-year, the team agreed to build a narrow-track car for McRae in time for New Zealand.

And he demonstrated the car's ability with a tremendous display of driving on the roads north of Wellsford. Going into the opening day's penultimate stage, he was already a minute up and laying solid foundations for possibly his biggest and best Kiwi win.

The leader wouldn't be coming out of Cassidy. The flat-four had fallen silent. And it wouldn't be the first time this year. Cambelt-related issues were the car's Achilles' heel and without them it's a fair assumption that Colin would justifiably have taken his second title in three years. That Subaru took its third title in three years came as little comfort to a man as competitive as McRae. Successive victories in Sanremo, Australia and Britain – with the car now on song – merely reminded the world what McRae was capable of.

By the end of the year, he and Prodrive had stopped seeing eye-to-eye on everything. The pupil had, it appeared, outgrown the teacher. There were talks with Ford, but the contract with Banbury was binding. McRae would stay.

On a personal level, 1997 was a life-changing year. He married Alison Hamilton, whom he had met via a friend of the family, on July 14.

## Monte Carlo Rally

January 17–23, 1997
Subaru Impreza WRC 97
Retired

The first time I sat next to Colin was on the Monte Carlo test and everything just clicked with the notes straight away, our relationship worked right from the word go. The 1997 Monte was memorable because there was a lot of snow that year and immediately I got a real grasp of Colin's driving style. One of the early stages saw us climb up a snowy mountain road with some big wide expanses to the side, which were parking areas normally used by skiers and coach parties. This uphill road had been perfectly ploughed and was really wide between the high snow banks. Then, after the col, the surface changed to wet, then dry tarmac. Colin had chosen a mixed tyre with some studs and went up the hill at full speed, chucking the car into these wide corners fully sideways. The spectators were going absolutely crazy, waving and shouting: "Yeeeeeeeeaaaasssssssssss!" I could tell he really enjoyed that. Unfortunately towards the end of that stage, Colin got caught out by a right-hander, we went off into the trees, ripped the front left wheel off and that was an instant retirement.

*Nicky Grist*

▲ McRae felt he could have won a nearly snowless Swedish in 1997, despite a pre-rally testing crash.

◄ Round-table geniality was tested after McRae felt Kenneth Eriksson gave him duff tyre information.

## Swedish Rally
February 8–10, 1997
Subaru Impreza WRC 97
Fourth

In December 1996, testing for the Swedish Rally, Colin became the first driver to roll a World Rally Car. On the actual rally there wasn't much snow around, just gravel and ice, and we were in a battle with our team-mate Kenneth Eriksson. Kenneth had done loads of testing with Pirelli and had come up with an idea for a half-buffed ice tyre with a short stud on the scrubbed portion of the tread. This made the tyre incredibly stable on the hard packed surface. We were up for winning this rally, so Kenneth didn't quite give Colin the full low down on this tyre set-up and went as far as putting him off using the buffed tyre for the last few stages. Kenneth, being Kenneth, took the special tyre for the final stages and absolutely thrashed us to win the rally. Colin was really upset about it, our Swedish Rally was gone and it could have been our first victory together. It was a lesson well learned. Previously, Colin had relied a lot more on other people and this was to be the start of him taking more notice, being a bit more alert and professional. There was a change in his approach after that rally.

*Nicky Grist*

# Safari Rally

March 1–3, 1997
Subaru Impreza WRC 97
First

I remember going to Kenya for the first time with Colin thinking that if there was one event that was definitely not an event for Colin McRae, it was the Safari Rally – only because of his reputation for being fast and aggressive. The Safari was a rally that needed to be driven more with your head than your foot, and when I looked at Colin's very basic pacenotes and compared them to Juha Kankkunen's, I could see that there was a lot of work to be done. During testing, we developed a descriptive note system, which included a speed for the corners with numbers one to six: six being the fastest. And a descriptive system for the rougher sections, including things like: fast, medium, bad and stop, and then things like: rocks, ditch, hole and so on. The benefit of this system was to allow Colin to drive as fast as he possibly could, yet slow enough that he was not going to damage the car.

This was the key to Colin winning the Safari Rally.

After the first day we were leading and Subaru were absolutely delighted because the Safari was more important to the Japanese manufacturers than just about any other rally; to win the Safari Rally meant your car was strong, fast and reliable. We set off north in the dark at five the next morning to service at Lake Naivasha, where the team nervously worked on the car at sunrise prior to the longest day of the rally. We had a new fitness coach called Bernie Shrosbree and his big thing was hydration, so he said to us: "Listen boys, you've got to hydrate today. It's gonna be hot so get plenty of fluids in."

We left service and at the start of the first stage of the day Colin said to me: "How much time have we got?" To which I had to tell him: "None, we've got to go now."

This first stage was 150 kilometres long and we nicknamed it 'The Road to Hell', because it was so bad in places – especially the first 40 kilometres, where we must have averaged only around 50kph driving along a destroyed railway line. After that we came onto a fast and wide dusty section that led to Elementita crossroads.

While doing about 160kph, Colin leaned across and said: "I need a piss."

There was no way we could afford to stop, so I told him to undo his trouser belt to relieve the pressure and concentrate on the driving.

"You'll be fine," I assured him.

We turned left at the crossroads and started to go uphill at high speed, bouncing over several rain gullies across the road until we arrived at the top and turned onto a short, but flat asphalt road. Colin accelerated through the gears until we were flat in sixth.

"Take the wheel," he shouted. "I can't hold it anymore!"

Colin undid his belts, jammed his right foot on the throttle and turned himself to the side, so he could pee out of the door. What he hadn't realised is that if you try to open a car door at over 160kph, you've got no chance. So he ended up having to pee against the inside door panel as we went through a long flat left and a long flat right, by which time he'd filled up the footwell.

There we were, flat-out, with my left hand on the wheel, people on pushbikes and donkeys at the side of the road and all the time I was conscious that coming up at the end of the asphalt was a series of big potholes before a village.

And Colin was still peeing.

At the last possible moment he fell into the seat, grabbed back the wheel and we went broadside through the village and continued on to the end of the stage. It turned out that Tommi Mäkinen had had six punctures in the stage and retired with broken transmission and we had actually set the fastest time by over three minutes…

*Nicky Grist*

Colin and Kenneth Eriksson's co-driver Staffan Parmander enjoy BAT's Safari Rally welcome party in The Carnivore restaurant, Nairobi.

Rally Catalunya 1997

Taking the slow boat to a fast rally. Colin and Nicky – along with other Subaru and Mitsubishi crews – pull their weight to make this Dragon Boat sing.

## China Rally

June 21–23, 1997
Subaru Impreza WRC 97
First

Colin didn't want to go to China for this Asia-Pacific round and did everything he could to persuade Prodrive not to send him. But this was the biggest market for our biggest sponsor (British American Tobacco's 555 brand) and they wanted Colin to do this rally. When he got there, he decided he was at least going to have some fun.

The Chinese authorities were very twitchy about the rally being there so we were given special driving licences and number plates that meant we could only drive our vehicles in the designated areas where the rally was. The recce was to be done in convoy with a police car up front, then the rally competitors lined up behind in car order number with the clerk of the course following to make sure everybody got through.

We were car number one and set off behind the police car. We passed by the Great Wall of China and just as we were about to turn north to the mountains, the police car suddenly turned the other way and went into a hotel car park. We stopped and waited for five minutes. With no reappearance of the police car, we decided to go off by ourselves. The officials didn't want us to loop around the

stages like we would normally do, but instead they planned for us to keep coming up and down the mountain and recce each stage individually, which would take ages. This was only day one of the recce and going up and down the mountain once was quite enough to do Colin's head in, so he said to me: "I've had a gutful of this already, get the map out, let's disappear. We'll do all the stages just the once so we can have tomorrow morning off."

Colin wanted a night out with our mechanics, so we headed straight for the Hard Rock Café in Beijing, where there was a promotion on that night, offering 25 per cent discount if you paid by VISA Gold card, so Colin and I treated the boys.

McRae had an absolute ball.

The next day, I was so ill that I was sick in a paddy field when we were completing our recce. Colin was just fine, he had an incredible constitution and he was never sick after alcohol.

*Nicky Grist*

## Rally Australia
October 30 – November 2, 1997
Subaru Impreza WRC 97
First

I knew Colin was faster than most drivers, but when it came to jumps nobody had more commitment than him. During the recce for Australia, we arrived at the famous Bunnings complex and Colin said: "These jumps are great!"

He made the pacenotes for the jumps in the way that a normal person would, so they read something like: "Caution. Five-right plus over bad jump, into six-left over jump, 60 crest…" The problem was, on the rally, the speed was so high leading up to the first crest that if you didn't slow down then anything could happen.

I remember hurtling into the first compression, taking off and being surprised how everything just went quiet. When we landed there was barely enough time to set up for the second jump, which we took sideways and I really jarred my back against the side of the seat on the landing after that one. We got through the watersplash, passed the flying finish, the crowd went wild and Colin turned to me and said: "Did ya like that, wee man?"

I tried to come up with something witty and clever to say and all I could manage was, "How high were we on those jumps? Gee-whiz, that was high, man. I've got a headache."

You had to expect Colin to come up with something spectacular and flamboyant because he was always the showman and that's what made people love him the world over. If he was spectating at Bunnings he would have loved seeing somebody jump as high as he did.

*Nicky Grist*

The most famous air in Australia. Nobody could touch McRae over the Bunnings jumps. Co-driver Nicky Grist was suffering altitude sickness when they landed!

## RAC Rally

November 23–25, 1997
Subaru Impreza WRC 97
First

This rally highlighted the different approach Colin had to Richard [Burns] when it came to making pace notes. Richard and his co-driver Robert Reid were quite intense in the way they planned things, they were methodical and Richard's pace notes were in-depth, containing every detail. For a magazine feature, Robert and I did a comparison of reading each other's notes for the same stretch of road and at literally the first corner, I got lost on Richard's notes.

Colin's read something like: "Long six-left opens," and that was it. For the same corner, Richard's read: "Flat-left, and flat-left-in, and flat-left."

Colin relied a lot on what he could see and feel, so if there was a flat-out kink in the road which he could see through then he wouldn't put it in the notes, whereas Richard would put it down as three straights and two very slight corners.

We were leading the rally after the Sunday stages, but Colin was really upset going into Radnor, the first stage on Monday morning because the organisers had the first car starting the stage at 0725, when daybreak was due around 0730. This meant later cars would progressively have the advantage of more daylight. We started the stage in total darkness. It was really foggy on the higher ground, there were some kinks on some of the straights and, as we just couldn't relate to where we were on the notes, we didn't know where the corners were. In the darkness Colin started turning the lights off, then on, then off again and the next minute we were off into a ditch. He floored the throttle, we popped back up on the road and that's when I said to him: "For fuck's sake! Either turn the lights on or turn the lights off, but let's concentrate and try to keep the car on the road or we'll be out of this rally."

We finished the stage and had lost a minute and a half to Richard. I just remember how angry and frustrated Colin was with the organisers, but by the end of the same day he had made up most of the time lost to Richard in Radnor.

Richard's notes were so precise, he could commit himself in fog a lot more than Colin. Richard relied on what heard from Robert whereas sometimes in Colin's career he relied more on what he could see.

*Nicky Grist*

RAC Rally hat-trick complete. McRae didn't compete in the non-championship event in 1996, and remained unbeaten at home since 1993. Incredibly, however, this would be his last home win.

# Mäkinen on McRae
## Fair and honest

Fair and honest. These two words are a running theme when Tommi Mäkinen is asked to describe Colin McRae as a competitor. And as a person, Tommi had real respect for Colin as well.

"Colin was a nice fella," says Mäkinen. "He was always straight up; when Colin wanted to point something out to you, he looked to your eyes in the conversation. And that was it. Case closed."

Mäkinen and McRae had some fierce fights. Australia, 1997 was a classic. And one that won't be forgotten. Tommi hit a tree on the fourth stage and dropped two minutes. But he fought back and was just 34 seconds behind Colin with two stages left. He was 21 seconds faster through the penultimate test. There was 30 kilometres to go and Tommi was 13 seconds behind.

"When Colin decided to fight," Mäkinen recalls, "he started to drive extremely fast. You had to really push if you wanted to respond, the pedal really had to be down – this was the only option."

Tommi won the Bunnings North stage by seven seconds but Colin won the rally by six.

"When we had a fight with Colin, the speed was phenomenal," says Mäkinen. "We drove on the edge and we both took huge risks. Quite often the result was that we both made mistakes and both had to retire. Look at our results, neither of us finished second very often…"

Colin was such a tough competitor because he was willing to push to the limit and over.

The four-time champion adds: "When the times got rough, Colin would never back off. His only target was to win the rally.

Finishing the rally was not the priority if there was a chance to fight for the victory."

And Mäkinen admits he couldn't always read the Scotsman's mind.

"He was like Kimi Räikkönen," says Tommi, "He was another iceman. You could never tell if he was under pressure. He just put the right foot down and drove. That's it."

Mäkinen's best scraps with McRae, according the Finn, were in Argentina, New Zealand and Indonesia.

"All the hardest battles took place on gravel," he says. "For some reason, I don't remember him being so much of a threat on asphalt."

Away from rallies, the two world champions were good friends with a common interest in enduro-biking.

"We used to take our motorbikes and go to the woods if we had a chance, we did this in Finland and in Spain after the recce," says Tommi. "It was always another good race. I miss these times. I was supposed to go over to Scotland to see him and his family at home, but it never happened. What happened in the end for Colin was terrible. He was my friend and I miss him. He was the good guy."

Between them, they dominated the WRC from the middle to late 1990s. Tommi had more titles, but Colin had more rally wins. Between them they picked up five championships and 49 outright rally wins. No driver was as spectacular to watch in that era as these two; Mäkinen and McRae were the masters of the final-stage fight.

Rally GB 2003 brought the curtain down on the full-time WRC careers of both Colin McRae and Tommi Mäkinen.

At Petter Solberg's wedding in 2003, McRae, Solberg and Mäkinen dressed up for the occasion. These three were the last men standing after the all-night party that followed.

Bagpipes play as Colin McRae and Tommi Mäkinen prepare for a superspecial showdown on the 1997 RAC Rally.

The legendary fight between McRae and Mäkinen on Rally Australia 1997 has passed into WRC folklore.

McRae

1998

It took time to sink in. After eight years of driving nothing but a flat-four, Colin McRae would be departing Subaru at the end of the year.

This move had been on the cards for some time. Having talked to Ford the previous season, McRae wasted no time in pursuing pastures new once he was out of contract.

Having been part of a winning team since 1994, this was the first season neither the Scot or Subaru took any silverware away from the FIA's end of season ceremony. The season started reasonably well and McRae's second successive Corsican win was enough to move him to the top of the table. And Finland was the only event of the remaining seven that he hadn't won before. The title looked very much alive.

Argentina provided a graphic demonstration of McRae's never-say-die attitude. Leading Tommi Mäkinen, Colin clobbered a rock near the end of Giulio Cesare, jamming a rear wheel into the arch. The suspension link was bent almost beyond conceivable repair. Almost.

McRae and Nicky Grist worked together, smashing the part between two rocks. In the end, they got it as straight as possible, bolted it back on and wheeled the crabbing Subaru quickest through El Condor. The win had gone, but two points were salvaged. An Acropolis win later and Colin was back to the front in the title race.

And then things started to slide, a puncture meant fifth in Auckland. Slapping the back of the Subaru against a tree rearranged the suspension into retirement spec in Finland. Sanremo brought some

respite with a fine recovery drive to edge Carlos Sainz for third after a puncture dropped him to 16th. By then, every point counted. With two rounds and 20 points on offer, McRae was eight off the front.

Australia decided it. Having never suffered a turbo failure on an Impreza rally car of any flavor, McRae's blower lunched itself right at the end of Bunnings. Had the turbo held on for just eight more kilometres, the end of season finale would have had a very different look. Colin would have been in the thick of the fight for the title on Rally of Great Britain.

As it was, that would just have made the end even harder to accept. And this was it. The end of the end.

On a rally which will forever be remembered for Sainz's heartbreaking engine problem at the end of Margam Park, McRaes time with Subaru was marked with a plume of blue smoke and a horrible rattle as it arrived at service in Builth Wells. He switched it off and the cowshed went silent.

That final rally had provided Colin with a unique opportunity, however, as his brother Alister joined him in the Subaru team. The McRae's started brilliantly, joint fastest – to the tenth of a second – on the opening stage. It didn't end quite the way it should have done. Alister was in the trees and Colin on his way to Ford.

A couple of weeks after that final appearance in blue, Colin and Alison's lives changed forever with the birth of their first child. Hollie Jane McRae was born on December 17, 1998.

World champion wheelman that he was, McRae was almost as capable under the bonnet. Here he inspects the flat-four with two Subaru Simons: Cole and Steele.

## Safari Rally

February 28 – March 2, 1998
Subaru Impreza WRC 98
Retired

Everybody remembers Colin for driving flat out and being on or over the limit all the time, but there was a surprising contradiction to the man. Because he was brought up with bikes and cars all his life, he did have amazing mechanical sympathy. Colin had a natural feel for what a car could take. He was generally our fastest driver, however his gearbox would come back in the best condition and he wasn't hard on the brakes. Tommi Mäkinen was very much the same, he and Colin could be aggressive and hard on their cars on a short sprint rally, yet they could get great results in Africa, where you might expect them to destroy a car after just 50 kilometres. Maybe because of all the enduro bike riding they had done they could both read a road fantastically well. They could see a smooth line through the rough places, but above all, they knew exactly what punishment a car could take.

*David Lapworth*

124

# Rally Argentina

May 20–23, 1998
Subaru Impreza WRC 98
Fifth

Unless you have driven the original gravel road from Mina Clavero up to the top of El Condor, it's hard to imagine just how narrow, twisty and rocky it really is. After the completely new asphalt pass was built, the old road was never maintained particularly well and when we drove it in 1998 it was in a pretty bad condition. There was one particular left-hander with a lot of exposed bedrock. Colin went steaming into sideways and whacked the back wheel hard against the rock. We finished the stage with the suspension so badly bent, we couldn't get the wheel off to fix it; the tyre was pushed hard up against the arch. Colin decided the best thing to do was to try to blow the tyre out of the arch. So he set off at speed down the asphalt road with smoke billowing out of the wheel arch. It worked and the tyre exploded – right in the path of a camera crew following us and filming the whole thing.

Once the wheel was off, we were committed to fixing the suspension geometry in order to continue and this brought out another side of

Colin McRae, a side not many people realised he had. Mechanically minded, he was one of the best guys around and he could lend his hand to fixing just about anything – because of the preparation work he did on his early rally cars. He stripped the rear down and got the suspension arm off, which had been bent through at least 40 degrees. We managed to straighten this arm by Colin holding it at each end and me smashing it with a huge rock that we'd found lying around next to the car. We put the car back together and managed to check into the famous El Condor stage with less than a minute to spare.

Colin's natural talent was such that, if there were a problem with the car, he would find a way to overcome it. We drove that stage and the next with the tracking way-out and yet we were fastest on both. Most drivers would have retired at the top of El Condor.

*Nicky Grist*

The lopsided right-rear wheel bears testament to the impact with a rock. The fastest times which followed bear testament to McRae's tenacity, resilience and mechanical ability.

The sign says it all. Greek fans adored Colin, who won their rally more times than anybody else. Some fans (the gentleman to the left of the shot) clearly loved Colin more than others...

## Acropolis Rally

June 7–9, 1998
Subaru Impreza WRC 98
First

Over the years the Acropolis was Colin's best event, albeit one you wouldn't have instinctively thought would be his type of rally. Prior to 1998, he'd already won it with Derek [Ringer], but this would be the first Acropolis I ever won. And, from start to finish, Colin drove the perfect rally. Little did I know that in years to come we would win that rally a further three times. I think Colin is as famous in Greece as he is in UK because of all those Acropolis victories. People love him there and you still see Greek rally fans with Colin McRae banners and flags, years after he died.

*Nicky Grist*

# China Rally

June 20–22, 1998
Subaru Impreza WRC 98
First

After all the fun he had in Beijing 12 months earlier, there probably wasn't too much persuading needed by BAT to get Colin on the entry list for the non-world championship 1998, 555-sponsored China Rally. This was a huge event for the tobacco giant and as McKlein was contracted as the official photographers there was plenty of work to be done. The event began with a lengthy and stereotypical ceremonial start in a football stadium, with lots of dragon dancing, after which various dignitaries flagged-off the rally cars in reverse order. The show would end with Colin McRae driving off the start ramp, cueing the beginning of a massive firework display. The organisers told me that they had spent € 50,000 on this single display, and in China that bought a LOT of fireworks. I asked Colin if he would mind not driving straight out of the stadium and back to his hotel, but rather stop his car, get out and watch the display. On the night both of the works Subaru crews were happy to oblige and the

result was a really good photograph. Colin was a great guy to work with and once he trusted you, nothing was ever a problem.

I don't remember much about Colin winning the 1998 China Rally, but I will never forget the flight home. After a big party the night before, Colin started drinking Bloody Marys with one of Prodrive's senior directors at Beijing airport. As soon as our British Airways 747 reached cruising altitude Colin downgraded himself from First to Economy class so he could continue to party with the Subaru boys. It was all good natured fun and when Colin decided he needed more spice in his tomato and vodkas, he procured the Tabasco sauce bottle from a stewardess, flicked out the plastic flow restrictor in its neck and then downed the whole bottle in one go. He did go a bit red in the face after that. I asked if he'd do it again, he just smiled and said, "Aye, nae bother!"

*Colin McMaster*

The sights and the sounds of a Chinese firework display. McRae and Liatti were more than happy to help McMaster with this long-exposure loveliness.

Sanremo Rally 1998

Rally Australia 1998

This puncture brought Colin and Nicky into close contact with the New Zealand constabulary.

## Rally New Zealand

June 24–27, 1998
Subaru Impreza WRC 98
Fifth

Punctures were really unexpected on New Zealand's smooth surface which was why, when we got one in 1998, we didn't have a spare. We set off down the public road to service in Otorohanga, driving on the wheel rim. We passed a Mitsubishi road car coming the other way and, unknown to us, something had flown off our car and smashed into this other car's windscreen. What we also didn't know was that the Mitsubishi was an unmarked police car – which turned around and set off after us.

Although our car only had three wheels, it's surprising how fast you can go in a World Rally Car and this policeman couldn't catch up with us, so he radioed ahead to get the police from Otorohanga to come out and stop us. The police pulled us over and eventually the Mitsubishi with the cracked windscreen arrived. The irate policeman

got out and started shouting at Colin, telling him he was going nowhere. Colin flew off the handle and started giving this policeman hell and I could see the way this situation was going, so I stepped in to calm it all down and get Colin to go back and sit in the rally car.

Diplomatically, I convinced the police that a three-wheeled World Rally Car, with its differentials locked has a lot more traction and braking capability than most road cars and that our mechanics, waiting in Otorohanga would return it to pristine condition in no time. So after a phone call to the chief of police, we were given the OK for a low-speed police escort along the hard shoulder all the way to service.

*Nicky Grist*

The end of the road. The smoking Subaru signals retirement from Rally GB.

# Rally of Great Britain

November 22–24, 1998
Subaru Impreza WRC 98
Retired

Colin stayed at Subaru for 1998, but the atmosphere was strained. Winning the manufacturers title was good for the team, but the driver's title meant everything to Colin. He felt mechanical failures had cost him the 1997 world championship and it's easy to understand how strained the relationship was. From around mid-season we started to hear rumours Ford wanted to sign Colin, and, although nothing was confirmed, it became clear that Colin and Nicky where ready to move on to pastures new.

The latter part of 1998 was quite difficult; Colin was excited about his new challenge and sometimes he made this very clear. We were sad to see him go given the history.

So, we came to the last rally, our home event, and it was a bad ending to one of the greatest partnerships in the WRC. A retirement with a blown engine, in a cattle shed in Builth Wells. Colin parked up, slammed the door shut and said: "That's that then." It kind of summed up a pretty glum mood by then.

*Alan McGuiness, Prodrive*

A sideways style meant McRae needed a clear view through the side windows.

Grist and McRae celebrate a multi million-dollar deal to move them from Subaru to Ford at the Dunton Technical Centre in Essex.

# **Colin** the family man

There were lots of girls who caught the attention of a teenage Colin McRae. But only one who held it. Alison Hamilton.

The pair met for the first time, through a friend of the family, when Alison was around 14. It's safe to say, love came at second sight. "I couldn't stand him!" says Alison, with a smile which hints at more to come. "I wasn't allowed to play on his Scalextric…"

Colin's mum Margaret wasn't fooled. "I knew," she said. "Once they started dating, I said to Jim: 'Alison's the one for Colin.' Maybe it took a wee while longer than expected, but they got there in the end."

Married on July 14, 1997, the honeymoon had to be shoehorned into a busy calendar of testing and rallies with the Subaru team. Colin, it appears, had two things to sort for the big day: his speech and the honeymoon. It seems he might have failed on both counts.

"I'd been on at him for weeks to get that speech written," says Margaret, "but he wouldn't, kept saying he'd be fine. Of course, he wasn't. He made a real backside of it and thanked *his* bridesmaids!"

A honeymoon starting in Fiji couldn't have been all bad… "It was a disaster!" recalls Alison. "Colin had called some guy he knew in Hong Kong to sort the hotel and when we got there it was damp, basic and filthy. I sat on the bed and cried. We'd passed a Sheraton on the way from the airport and fortunately they had a beautiful room spare, so we took that."

Just over a year into married life, Hollie was born, with her younger brother Johnny arriving three years later. The family was complete. And, when Colin found himself without a full-time drive in 2004, Alison looked forward to their lives ahead. She says: "I remember thinking how the hard work was done and Colin was going to be home more from now on. It was time to really enjoy life. I get angry about things sometimes, but then I remember the laughs and the memories and how fortunate I was to have them. I remember Colin as the love of my life, my first and only love and Hollie and Johnny's Dad. I miss life as it should be."

The McRae girls remember a pair of boys who loved life, mixed with mischief and full of fun. "Johnny was so competitive," says Alison. "And he would run around all day, skidding and kicking up stones like he was a rally car. Sometimes he'd have these big falls in the yard and I was like: "Oh my God!" but he'd get straight up and carry on. He was really shy, but really dignified – he always had his shirt buttons done up and looked smart."

Hollie remembers a universal approach to bike riding lessons. She says: "Dad was teaching me to ride a bike one day and he thought he'd just teach Johnny at the same time. So he took the stabilisers off both our bikes and shouted: "Just go for it!" Then there was the time he lifted us both up to hold onto one of the beams in the house and then pretended to leave us hanging there!"

The bond between Hollie and Johnny was as strong as any sibling. Must have been: Hollie was the only one who could get Johnny to touch his homework.

"I used to say: "Come to the play room and we'll take this bowl of chocolates…" Hollie says. Such was the richness of life in the McRae household, that when it came to bedtime stories, Enid Blyton was put to one side. "Dad would always tell us great stories about things that had happened," says Hollie. "Telling us about boats that

sank or skiing trips that went wrong. There was always a story. And I love to hear those stories from Gramps (Jim) now.

"I like to remember Dad just the way he was… the big, friendly family man."

Alison and Colin's wedding day on July 14, 1997. It's all smiles before touchdown in Fiji.

## » **Memories of Colin**

I remember getting one of those Disney cheque books when I was younger. You could write a cheque out to somebody telling them they could always get a hug when they felt sad. I wrote one of those out to Dad, it was a cheque with the Disney character Goofy on it, and I said: "You can always goof around with me…" That's why I remember Dad as Goofy!

*Hollie McRae*

In Spain 2001, Colin McMaster enlisted Hollie McRae's help to assist Dad in a photoshoot for a sunglasses sponsor.

Monaco 2000. Father and daughter exchange a kiss with Uncle Alister in the background.

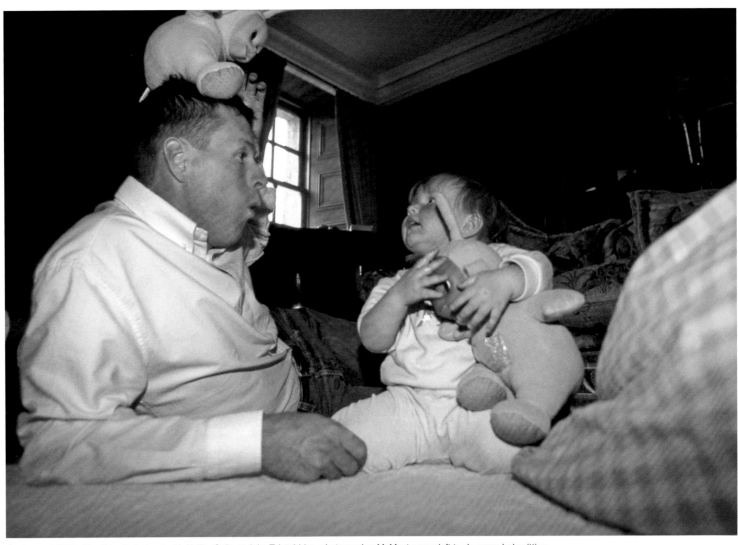

Jerviswood 1999. After this photoshoot with Hollie, Colin and the Teletubbies, photographer McMaster was left to do some babysitting.

Colin and Alison, China 1998.

Colin and son Johnny relaxing together aboard Sea Mac, the McRae boat on which Colin loved to spend his downtime.

The look says it all: Colin and Alison made a great couple.

These two 'birds' turned a few heads at the 1996 Prodrive Christmas party.

Colin, Alison and a 13-month old Hollie pose for a family photo at the start of the 2000 Monte Carlo Rally.

McRae

**1999**

1968-1984 | 1985-1986 | 1987-1990 | 1991 | 1992 | 1993 | 1994 | 1995 | 1996 | 1997 | 1998 | **1999** | 2000 | 2001 | 2002 | 2003 | 2004 | 2005 | 2006 | 2007

The Autosport Show in the second week of the New Year brought realisation that the move really had happened. For the first time in his full-time world championship career, Colin McRae was not wearing the iconic blue and yellow threads which he'd looked so comfortable in for the last six of his eight years with Subaru.

But he'd replaced them with something equally iconic: the red, white and blue of Martini. Colin, the forever Subaru man had left Banbury for a clean sheet of paper with Ford. And it was the same story with Ford as the Blue Oval turned its back on the Escort – a car which had served it exceptionally well for 25 years – in favour of the Focus.

Having been talking to Malcolm Wilson on and off since 1997, the two-year deal was signed on August 5, 1999. McRae's 31st birthday was not one he would forget for a while – it's not every birthday you sign a contract worth in excess of £6 million.

Ford had hoped Juha Kankkunen would partner McRae, but he went in the opposite direction and arrived at Subaru. The upshot of that was unquestioned number one status in the team for Colin, but also an awful lot of testing work on a brand new car for him to shoulder. Pre-season testing came and went in a flash and a change of team didn't bring a change of fortune in Monte Carlo. Prior to the debut of Ford's Focus WRC, the car failed scrutineering due to an irregularity with the water pump. The team started and ran under appeal, confident in their case. Four stages in and the dream was realised, Malcolm Wilson's all-new car driven by Ford's all-new driver was fastest. McRae ended the event third. Briefly. Exclusion hit hard for the Scot, who thought the dice might finally have fallen in his favour in Monte Carlo.

The M-Sport team re-worked the engine bay of the Focus in time for Sweden and on round two, Ford kept its third place – this time taken by McRae's team-mate Thomas Rådström. Colin retired on day two with headgasket failure.

Having been unsure whether the team would make it to Sweden. And then having been unsure whether to let the cars start once they had made it to Sweden, the Safari was a real mountain for Ford and McRae to climb on round three.

But every now and then, the unthinkable happens. And, by the time the rally rode across the equator on day two, the Ford was in the lead. And it stayed there, demonstrating solid reliability and durability – two of the three core principles Wilson had wanted the car built on.

Just under a month later, in Portugal, the third principle was firmly established with the car's first win on a European sprint event.

The World Rally Championship collectively took a breath. Here was a team with a new driver and completely new car taking two wins from the first four rounds. Before Monte, there had been contemplation that maybe a win or two might be possible in the second half of the season, but championship talk was on hold for a year.

Four rounds in and McRae was just two points behind Tommi Mäkinen.

Unfortunately for the new pairing, that was as close as they would get to challenging for season-long glory throughout the rest of the year. There would be just one more result in 1999, a fourth-place in Corsica. China delivered the team's biggest blow, when both McRae and Rådström retired side-by-side having hit the same rock on the first stage.

Mid-way through the year, Colin drove a Focus as course car on his own rally in southern Scotland. Tens of thousands of fans turned out to watch one car, confirming that world rallying's most expensive man still had the same draw in a Ford as he'd enjoyed in a Subaru.

His second trip home didn't bring quite the same enjoyment. Having just endured a terrifying 160kph crash in Australia, McRae went off the road slightly slower, but with similarly rally-ending results in Myherin, Wales. His British rival Richard Burns went on to win his second successive Rally GB.

McRae's first season with Ford had delivered hope and glory, grounded with plenty of realism. While he was never really in with a shot at the title, commercially speaking 1999 was another big step forward for the McRae brand. He'd featured in a Ford television commercial and sales of his eponymous computer game were going through the roof.

A new beginning, but the same old luckless story in Monte. McRae and the all-new Focus WRC stunned in the Alps, but were excluded for a water pump indiscretion.

## Monte Carlo Rally

January 17–21, 1999
Ford Focus WRC
Disqualified

At the time I thought it was a risqué move for Colin going from Subaru to Ford for 1999. The first time Colin and I went to see the car, it was in a workshop Ford had rented at Millbrook in late 1998. The Focus was nowhere near finished, but we were due to go testing in mid-December.

We didn't do much mileage in the Monte test, because the weather conditions were really bad and there were problems with the car. Initially, Ford had big problems with the Focus suspension because the springs were too stiff and Colin wasn't happy with the car. He complained about the handling and, just as we were about to start changing things, the car caught fire because of a hydraulic leak and our test was over. We flew home for Christmas, but because everything was running so late we were back out testing before New Year. That was cut short too because the power steering blew up, so we went home and were back out again after New Year.

When we eventually started the rally, the first stage was 50 kilometres. We only got about 10 kilometres in before we had to stop the car – we were choking from smoke inside. As an indication of how little testing we'd done, the heat from the exhaust was burning the paint inside on the floorpan of the car and this fire had to be put out with the extinguisher before we could keep going. We eventually finished third on that first event with Ford, but we were then excluded.

*Nicky Grist*

## Swedish Rally

February 11–14, 1999
Ford Focus WRC
Retired

Colin was shocked with Thomas Rådström's speed in Sweden. We went out testing the day before the rally started and Colin stood and watched. After Thomas and I drove past him, he said that was unbelievable to watch. He had no answer to Thomas in Sweden.

*Fred Gallagher*

The blue and yellow were binned for Martini's red, white and blue in 1999.

# Safari Rally

February 25–28, 1999
Ford Focus WRC
First

Each time I've been to Kenya, a great friend of mine called Jan Thoenes has taken me to the Muthaiga Club for lunch, where we would have a few bottles of wine and maybe the odd Calvados afterwards. In 1999 Jan came to meet me at the Ford team hotel and, as we were about to leave, Thomas, Nicky and Colin turned up. Before I could say anything, Jan had invited them along too and I knew it would end in tears. The Muthaiga Club is a members only club where you can't spend cash, so poor old Jan was signing chitty after chitty as we all had a fair bit of wine before heading to the bar at about 1700, where we had more drinks. In the taxi back to the hotel, there was a fair bit of banter going on and I was giving Colin some stick about Thomas and I blowing him away in Sweden. I was sat in the front seat with Colin behind and he reached forward to give me a huge bear-hug, which cracked three of my ribs. When we got back to the hotel I went straight to my room to try and sleep things off, unaware of the chaos going on downstairs.

I was woken when the team doctor phoned. He said: "We've got a problem... Thomas has broken his leg!"

As Thomas was weaving his way to reception to get his key to go to bed, McRae decided he would rugby tackle him. Colin gave him a full rugby tackle and Thomas went down on a marble floor and that was that: his leg was hanging at 90 degrees.

We all convened in Colin's bedroom, shitting ourselves that we would lose our jobs. We hushed the story up to an extent and agreed that we should say that Thomas had slipped on some paint. Malcolm Wilson came on the phone to me at about two in the morning and told me Petter Solberg was flying out to take Thomas' place and that I was going to co-drive for him. We did do a fantastic job and the fact that Colin won and that Petter and I were fifth made a massive difference for Malcolm. But it wasn't until 2009 that I told him the whole story of what happened to Thomas in Kenya.

*Fred Gallagher*

This was only the third ever event for the Focus and nobody believed you could take a new car to the Safari Rally and win first time out. Even on the last day of the rally Carlos Sainz said to me: "When's that Focus going to break?"

You would think it was out of character for Colin to go and win the Safari, but he just had this ability to understand exactly the level of punishment a car could take on a rough event like that. He knew that speed was not the ultimate factor for winning; it was mechanical sympathy and he understood it. This was a fantastic start to our relationship. When we signed Colin, we knew what we'd signed up for: great victories and some mistakes too.

*Malcolm Wilson*

An emotional – and almost unbelievable – first win for Ford was delivered on the most testing rally of them all in Kenya.

## Rally of Portugal
March 23–26, 1999
Ford Focus WRC
First

We saw the true Colin in Portugal. He took 31 seconds out of every competitor in the first three stages by driving flat-out. From then on, we were able to control the rally.

*Malcolm Wilson*

As a brand, Ford was really trying to promote the Focus, but they'd made no provisions in the press to advertise the fact that they'd won the toughest rally of the lot on the Safari. Next up was the Rally of Portugal, a sprint event and lo and behold we went and won that as well. But, again Ford had no advertising booked, nothing was prepared, so promoting another victory went by the wayside. After Portugal, Ford made provisions for the rest of the year to produce success ads… but, apart from Corsica, we retired on all the other events!

*Nicky Grist*

# Tour de Corse

May 7–9, 1999
Ford Focus WRC
Fourth

If it wasn't for Colin, I wouldn't be where I am today. I learned so much – good and bad things – from him. He was helpful, generous and respectful. But he also gave me some shit because I asked a lot of questions. He would tell me to shut up. But, after five minutes, I'd ask him again, so he had no choice but to tell me the answers.

Colin and I would drive together on the recces, which we did in Corsica in 1999. That time, I had a turbo diesel Golf road car and he had the proper Ford Escort Cosworth recce car. We had a competition to see if I could keep up with him on a stage. He never thought I would be able to do it, but because of the torque – ideal for a road full of corners – I was pushing his ass all the way!

*Petter Solberg*

◀ Fred Gallagher displays a retirement form filled out for both Fords, which retired in the same corner of China.

▼ Mutual misery for Grist and Gallagher. A Beijing night out cheered them up.

# China Rally
September 16–19, 1999
Ford Focus WRC
Retired

Colin had had a difficult run up to this event and all the talk was about how it'd all gone wrong for McRae? After the recce we were fairly confident and knew that a steady run would pay off on a tough event, which was new for everyone.

When Thomas Rådström and I started the first stage, we'd only done about 500 metres when we saw Colin's car facing us far up the hill ahead. We couldn't believe it and had time to express to each other how incredible it was that Colin had gone off so early in the event.

Not pushing hard and following the lines of the preceding cars, we suddenly heard a bang and hit the same stone that Colin had. We spun around and as if we were formation auto-testing, came to a stop with the nose of our car up against the tail of his. The same part had broken on both cars and that was it, both were out.

We were all really fed up with the situation and the local Chinese food was getting to us, so we decided we were going to Beijing for a night out. Malcolm Wilson had other ideas. The Focus was going to be driven up and down that same section of stage until the problem was sorted out. And since Thomas had misbehaved in Kenya he would be the one to miss the party and do the driving!

So Colin, Nicky and I bade him farewell and went out for a night at the Hard Rock Café, in the civilisation of Beijing. The food tasted great after ten days out in the sticks and the cold beers flowed well. But, when Colin asked the waitress to bring an ice-bucket to our table, and to fill it with a bottle of vodka instead of white wine I remembered Nairobi, made my excuses and left!

*Fred Gallagher*

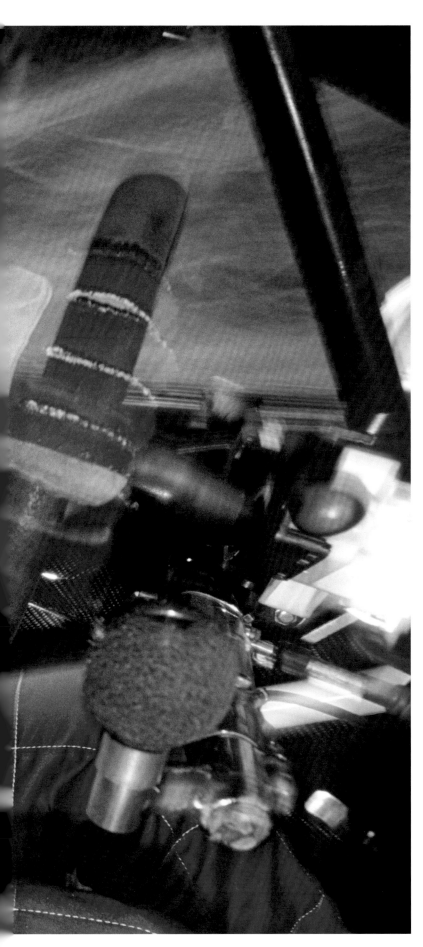

## Rally Finland

August 20–22, 1999
Ford Focus WRC
Retired

We had some engine problems, which eventually burned a hole in a piston, which meant we were pumping gallons of oil into the car just to keep it going. The last stage of the rally was a special live television stage, for which the top three were awarded extra points. Unfortunately for Ford, the engine expired in a big way, right on top of one of the biggest crests in Finland, in front a huge crowd and on live television. We were 400 metres from the finish, but we were going no further.

*Nicky Grist*

## Rally Australia
November 4–7, 1999
Ford Focus WRC
Retired

Colin's nickname was 'McCrash' but despite what some people think, when you sat in a car with him, it wasn't a case getting round one corner and thinking: "Oh shit, here comes the next one…" Colin was a fast, but very confident driver. When we were on-song, there was no better feeling than sitting next to him, the adrenaline rush and the buzz of it all was absolutely stunning. There were times when he tried to take it that little bit further, you would go a tiny bit wide, clip something or even hit something. We had a few fairly monstrous accidents, but Australia, 1999, was the only time I thought: "I'm dead."

We were going through a fast, wide section, which was followed by a right-hander taken flat in sixth gear. At this point, the road passed a junction coming in from the left. We were using the old notes from the previous year, but they had re-graded the road from this junction on the left, creating a bump on the stage, which made the car jump. The pacenotes now said: "Six right, over jump."

On the rally I remember coming into this corner and Colin, as always, was totally committed. The car just launched itself in the air sideways, and came down hard on the front left wheel, with such a force that it wrenched the steering wheel out of Colin's hands. The car was disappearing broadside off to the left and I was staring at

the biggest tree I've ever seen in Australia – it must have been at least five foot round. And it was coming straight for my side window. People say that, just before you die, your whole life flashes before your eyes; it's remarkable that it did for me. I was thinking about Shaz [Sharon Grist, Nicky's wife], my family and my friends. At the last moment, I shut my eyes waiting for the impact. I remember hearing the crunch, feeling the car spinning around and having a pain in my foot. When everything stopped, I opened my eyes and thought: "Christ, I'm alive!"

In those last few feet the car must have changed direction a wee bit and, fortunately, instead of hitting my door, the impact with the tree came just behind the front wheel, where the windscreen pillar and engine were. It destroyed the engine and gearbox and my toe was broken where my foot had smashed against the roll-cage.

Afterwards, Colin admitted he thought he was going to die as well. In every other big accident we had after that one, Colin either emerged unscathed or he hurt himself, but that was the only time I ever hurt myself with Colin.

*Nicky Grist*

148

# Rally of Great Britain

November 21–23, 1999
Ford Focus WRC
Retired

After the big crash in Australia, we went to Rally of GB where there was a big hype in the press about the battle between Colin and Richard Burns. In the classic McRae years, it was only the win in 1997, where I remember finishing that rally. Whatever happened it was usually a pretty bad event for him. Colin won all the PR wars with Richard, but [on rally GB] he'd always try too hard, too soon, and end up doing something stupid.

In 1999, we were in the second run through Myherin, in the dark. On one particularly long right-hander, which continued over a crest – where there was a 50-metre clearing of trees – there was a car on the left hand side, which had gone off on the first run. When McRae came to the crest he must have thought the road was going somewhere else and he tried to drive around the other car, which launched us into the tree stumps and we were out. It was a classic situation where most other drivers would lift-off or brake.

*Nicky Grist*

McRae

2000

1968-1984 1985-1986 1987-1990 1991 1992 1993 1994 1995 1996 1997 1998 1999 **2000** 2001 2002 2003 2004 2005 2006 2007

The second season. The championship year. That was the plan. And there was an old friend back alongside Colin in the team. Carlos Sainz rejoined Ford for 2000.

Boarding the plane to depart Cyprus in September, things were looking good for Colin and Ford. Granted, there had been frustrations earlier in the season, but they were second in the title race, just two points behind Marcus Grönholm. It didn't take long for things to go wrong.

Typically, the year had started with disappointment in Monte Carlo, when the engine went bang, but McRae finished a rally for the first time in 10 starts when he took third in Sweden.

The next four events brought three more retirements and one win. There was speculation that the Scot would walk away. He had reportedly talked to Peugeot and Subaru – where a potential British super-team of Burns and McRae was in David Richards' mind. McRae, however, could see the potential with M-Sport's Ford. And mid-season pace and consistency delivered another win (albeit an orchestrated victory over Carlos Sainz which briefly re-opened Catalan wounds from 1995), three second places and another two-year contract with Ford.

Then came Corsica.

If Colin had, fleetingly, thought he was going to die in Australia at the end of 1999, that idea remained at the forefront of his mind for far too long on Saturday, September 30. Running fourth, Colin went into a long left-hander too quickly. What followed was a horrible, calamitous chain of events. The Focus rolled, roof-first through a Focus-sized hole in the wall, and dropped, roof-first again, into a Focus-sized hole 10 metres below the road.

The Ford came to rest upside down, Colin and Nicky hung in their belts; only the Welshman was conscious and able to move. Above them, cars came and went. Nobody stopped, nobody helped. Why would they? Skid marks on the road indicated little more than a moment on the road close to Corte.

Colin eventually came around, but when he did, he woke to a living nightmare. Upside down, unable to move, in terrible pain from facial injuries and, just when things couldn't get any worse, fuel was leaking from the car. The emergency services came, but were able to offer little help in such a specialised situation. In the end, Ford's fitness trainer Bernie Shrosbree, engineer Martin Wilkinson and Colin's father Jimmy arrived on the scene to direct the rescue. After 50 minutes, Colin was freed from the car and on his way to hospital.

Ten days after an operation to repair a shattered cheekbone, Colin was back in the car in Sanremo. At the time he admitted he'd been ready to knock it all on the head. But ahead of Italy, he was still only four points off the front…

Colin showed unbelievable bravery to get into the car, let alone finish sixth overall to take a championship point. More importantly, his cheekbone remained intact. Having demonstrated such mental and physical fortitude, it was ironic that McRae's title chance was lost when his Ford suffered a piston failure on a road section in Australia. A second Welsh accident in succession ensured a miserable end to what had been another difficult season for Colin. But one he fully appreciated could have been a lot worse.

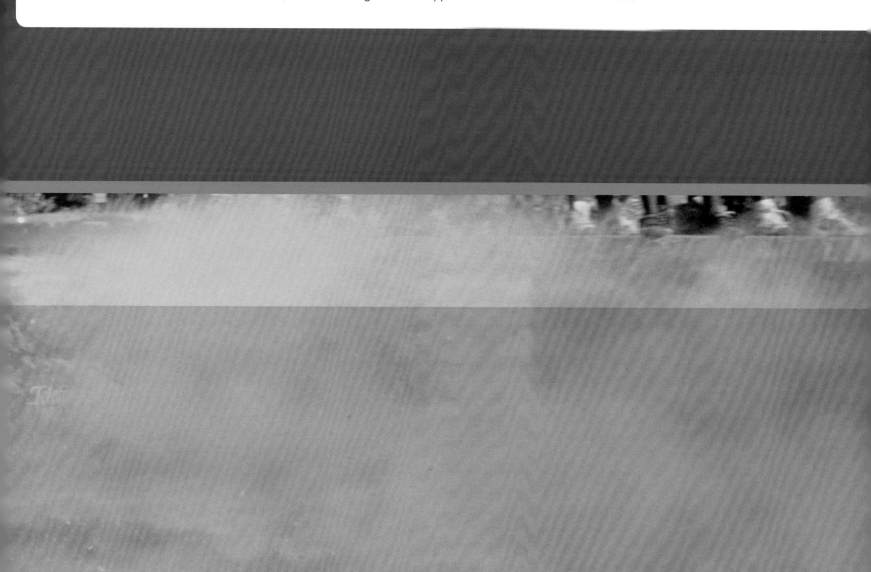

## Rally Catalunya

March 31 – April 2, 2000
Ford Focus WRC
First

The car had a clutch problem leaving service which meant that Colin had to affect the repairs himself. There was nobody better to have on the tools than Colin, at our Christmas parties he would always challenge the technicians that he could do the jobs quicker than they could.

*Malcolm Wilson*

The Mendensita jump provided the perfect opener for Autosport's report on the 2000 Acropolis – an event which re-opened old wounds between McRae and Sainz when the Spaniard was told to finish second.

## Acropolis Rally

June 9–11, 2000
Ford Focus WRC
First

When I do after-dinner speeches, I'll talk about this jump – it was mental. It was near the end of the Mendensita stage and, when I try to describe it, I tell people that if you put a car in the bottom of the dip between the two crests, you wouldn't see the car as you approached the first crest. That's how deep it was. From crest-to-crest must have been about four car lengths. On the recce Colin stopped, had a look at it and said: "I think we can jump this." We all had GPS tracking on our recce cars so the organisers could see we weren't breaking the recce speed limit of 80kph, so there was no way we could check this jump at proper speed. Undeterred, Colin had another idea. "I know," he said, "we'll get my Dad to come and check it…"

So the next day, Jimmy McRae and Campbell Roy took the recce car to this jump and tried it at speed. Jimmy took off on the first crest and landed nose-first into the second, ripping the front off the Escort Cosworth and doing around £4,000 worth of damage. When Jimmy eventually came back he reckoned that Colin would be carrying a lot more speed in the rally car and would probably make the jump.

On the rally we were in a big battle with our team-mate Carlos Sainz. When we arrived at the start of the Mendensita stage, I asked Colin what we were going to do on this jump and he said: "I don't know, I'll see how I feel when I get there." I knew that if he tried and we didn't make it, it would be a case of 'Goodnight Irene.' When we got to the crests I read the pacenotes as normal. I was expecting some big braking, Colin to change down a couple of gears, go down into the dip and up the other side. But no, he just kept his foot down and I thought: "Oh Christ, hold on tight – he's gonna jump it."

The front of the car took off, but the back was kicked up in the air as it hit the top of the crest. We cleared both crests, just, and, after we landed, knowing the stage was to be re-run in the afternoon, I said: "That was a bit dodgy, best not do that again." Colin, completely unfazed, replied: "No, no, no, it's fine. I took it too much to the left. We'll take it more to the right this afternoon."

That jump was a classic case of Colin thinking differently to the rest, seeing something that nobody else could see and being willing to try it.

*Nicky Grist*

Cyprus Rally 2000

## Rally New Zealand
July 13–16, 2000
Ford Focus WRC
Second

He was so desperate to win. It wasn't a case of win or crash, with Colin there was nothing in between. He just wasn't happy finishing second.

*Malcolm Wilson*

# Tour de Corse

September 29 – October 1, 2000
Ford Focus WRC
Retired

Colin's wins in Corsica in 1997 and 1998 were two of his best. He wasn't scared of the place and he made it his own in those years, which was really quite rare for a rally usually dominated by the French.

All that was about to change after 2000.

The crash came on a new stage, just south of Corte and, unusually for Corsica, it included a section which was flat-out for a kilometre and a half. The pacenotes read something like: "… long five-right, 50, long six-left and six-left 30, three-left, two-right…" Of course, fives and sixes were pretty much flat-out, and 30 metres after the six-left, we had a third-gear left-hander into a second-gear right. I remember we were flying along and all of a sudden, out of nowhere it seemed, came the third-gear left; Colin hadn't even lifted off the throttle. The corner narrowed to go over a bridge and there was a steep bank on the inside, where the road went close to the rock-face.

We were going miles too fast, so Colin pitched the car in early to try to give himself some more space. We hit the banking on the inside. The car began to corkscrew in the air, before going through a stone-wall on the outside of the bridge. There was a gap in the wall, which our car fitted through perfectly, on its side. We then plunged down into the ravine below, whacking into a massive tree which pierced the windscreen on Colin's side.

When the noise stopped, we were upside down and 10 metres down in the ravine in complete darkness. I put my hand down, undid my belts and asked Colin if he was all right. He didn't reply. There was silence. He was unconscious. When you're upside down in a situation like that, you get completely disorientated – you don't know where anything is. I tried to open my door, but I couldn't, it was wedged against something. The gap was too small to get out. I took my helmet off and I lay on my back on the roof, trying to kick my way out.

Then Colin came round and he was screaming at me to get him out. All I could say was: "You're OK. I'm here and I'll get you out." I managed to squeeze my way out and when I went round the back of the car to get to Colin I could see that there was petrol dripping out. The driver's door just fell off in my hands, revealing instantly what had happened to Colin. The force of hitting the tree had pushed the roof and windscreen pillar down all the way over his face and the steering wheel was buckled into his chest. All I could see of his face was one side of his cheek and there was blood dripping from that.

I got the jack out to try and open up the space between the floor and the roof to give him some more room, but it didn't work. A few cars had passed on the stage above, but nobody stopped because there wasn't a single sign of any wreckage on the road and we hadn't left a mark on the wall either. There were no spectators around, there was no radio reception and I needed help. I decided to run about a kilometre to the nearest radio point to get the marshals there to stop the stage and get some emergency vehicles to Colin. I telephoned the Ford team in service to let them know the situation and immediately Jimmy McRae and Bernie Shrosbree set off in the recce car to get to the scene.

Eventually, when the first help did arrive it was the local minor fire services and they were not used to dealing with roll-cages, bucket seats and such like. I left it to who I thought were the experts, but it didn't look right to me – they didn't know what to do and there was only one medical guy and he was standing on the car's underside,

putting more force down on Colin. After about 30 minutes, the Corsican rescue operation came to a complete stop.

Jimmy and Bernie had arrived and we had to take control of the situation. The only way to get Colin out was to try and flex the car open and make some space. We got the guy with the cutters to chop off the steering wheel, then chop some of the roll cage in order to free up the bodyshell. Because Bernie is built like the proverbial brick shithouse, I got him to stand on the roof with his hands on the doorsill and prize the car open. I went back inside the car and put my feet on the floor with my back against the transmission tunnel and tried to help. Working in tandem, the pair of us managed to open up enough space so that the others could slowly start to manoeuvre Colin out. All the while, petrol was still coming out the back of the car.

We got Colin out of there in about 50 minutes. When they put him on a stretcher I had never seen anybody looking so ill in all my life, he was a horrible grey colour. His face was really badly swollen on one side and that was where the roof had cut his skin and smashed his cheekbone. That was probably the only time when Colin's life was in serious danger in a rally car.

Out of all his accidents, I think this is the one that really did stick in Colin's mind. It shocked him quite badly. He couldn't remember anything about the crash and although the stage wasn't used the following year, we took the notes and revisited the scene to drive the road again. The accident was caused by a mistake in the notes where we had: "… long six-left and six-left 30…" In reality, there was no second six-left – he'd added it in. So he was driving flat out waiting for a six left, when he should have been braking for the third-gear left-hander coming up in 30-metres.

*Nicky Grist*

I'd had a dream the night before that one of the boys had crashed and I didn't know which one of them it was. I'd never been to Corsica before, but from the moment I landed I had this feeling. The morning of the accident, I remember telling Jim: "I had this terrible dream last night, one of the boys crashed…" Jim asked me which one it was and I didn't know. But the minute the service park went quiet after the crash, I knew. I didn't know which one it was, but I knew it was one of mine.

After the accident, when he was in the hospital, I thought he was taking the Michael; he kept saying: "Did I win the rally?" and we would tell him he'd had an accident, but he was fine. He'd drift off, come around and say: "Did I win the rally?"

I just knew there was something going to happen on that event. When he came back from Corsica and landed at home, Alison was there to pick him up from the airport and, even though they had been married for three years, that was the first time I got the feeling that Colin wasn't my boy anymore.

*Margaret McRae*

Nicky called me. I knew something was wrong. "Martin," he said, "you need to get here."

I jumped in the car and headed up to the stage. When we got there, it was obvious that the organisers were panicking. Nobody was taking charge of the situation. When I looked down on the car, I couldn't think of anywhere worse to have a crash.

This was hell.

When I got down to the car, there was water running through it. It was upside down, and there was a stream running along the inside of the roof – it was just deep enough to be touching the top of Colin's crash helmet. And you could smell the fuel. And see it. The leaking fuel was sitting on top of the water and spreading. The whole place could have gone up in an instant. All the time we were working down there I really thought the place was going to be up in flames in a moment. It was a nightmare, knowing that Colin was trapped in there and that we could all be about to go in a flash with a big explosion.

Bernie [Shrosbree] was great. He'd been in emergency situations before and dealt well with it. One of the worst things about this whole thing was that we couldn't see Colin's face. He was trapped in the car by his face. We held his hand and we could touch his leg, but that was all.

I was working with the firemen, telling them where it was safe and where it was best to cut through the cage. In the end, Bernie was in the car pulling the cage off Colin's face.

Finally, we got him out. He was such a mess. I remember thinking when I saw him: "Well, that's him finished." I just didn't see how he could have come back from that.

There's no doubt, that was one of the most horrific experiences of my life. It was hellish. Words alone can't come close to describing just how bad that afternoon was.

*Martin Wilkinson, Ford World Rally Team engineer*

## » Memories of Colin

Colin was a free spirit, he was my big hero and he still is. Colin could drive a good car fast but he could also drive a bad car fast too. He could do some extraordinary things at times, like damage his car and then go and set the fastest time on the next stage with that damaged car. It wasn't just rally cars with Colin; he could pick up anything mechanical and immediately get the best out of it. He could get on a jet ski for the first time and, straight away, be quicker than somebody who had been doing it for ages. The same applied with a motocross bike, a road bike or even skis. I remember when we both bought Yamaha 450cc bikes and took them to a rally test. I'd had mine for a couple of months but Colin's was brand new, so I knew the bike more than he did. This was my chance to impress him. When we set off I pulled a wheelie and held it in first, then second gear, for about 50-metres. Just as I dropped down the front wheel, Colin passed me in third gear on his back wheel and then changed up to fourth. He had been on that bike for less than five minutes. That was Colin.

*Christian Loriaux*

Grip is of paramount importance on the Western Australian ball-bearings – as McRae's shunt in this part of the world 12 months earlier testified – Colin and Nicky swap fronts for rears.

# Burns and McRae

## Rivals

by David Evans

Chalk. Cheese. Fire. Ice. Pick your analogy. McRae and Burns couldn't have met at the top via more different routes. But, for a while, a cruelly short while, Britain had it better than any other nation. And the British media had it better than anybody. The battle of the Brits was a story which just kept on giving.

Retrospectively and quite correctly, much is made of the friendship which emerged and endured from Britain's two best rally drivers ever. But, at the time, the competition was white-hot and the needle between the pair absolutely for real.

For McRae, Burns was an upstart. He'd been Subaru's junior in the Scot's 1995 title-winning year and before that, a rival for his younger brother Alister. Colin was on top of the world and, as far as he was concerned, there was only room for one top Brit. And he was there.

Typically, Richard had taken his time in building his career. A period at Mitsubishi had given him solid foundations from which to build on and, by the time he returned to Subaru to replace Colin for 1999, he was a force to be reckoned with.

The pair couldn't have been more different in their approach and early years in the sport. Colin took the limit and vaulted it in a big gear. When he crashed, he'd come back and have another go; a fraction less throttle this time. And he'd do that until he got over the jump or through the corner. He might have bashed panels to get there, but when he went through that corner and over that jump he did so faster and further than anybody else. That left McRae with absolute self-belief that he was the fastest driver in the world.

Richard eyed the limit respectfully. And approached it from a very, very fast and competent base level, getting quicker and quicker until he was confident he was getting the most from himself and his machinery. His natural talent, allied to that learning experience, dictated that, at the turn of the Millennium, he was a match for McRae.

In New Zealand, 2001, Richard scored a big win against Colin, beating him in the kind of final-day showdown which the Scot rarely lost (and had beaten Richard too, as recently as Argentina earlier that season). Three rounds later and the pair went to Rally GB separated by just two points as part of a four-way title showdown. Fleet Street melted.

Colin's move was immediate. The speed he showed through St Gwynno was nothing short of breathtaking; the Focus was a gear-up in most corners. This couldn't carry on. Could it?

No.

Richard took a tenth on Tyle and that was it, McRae was ready to settle this one. He redoubled his efforts in Rhondda and, after cutting a right-hander against the advice of his co-driver Nicky Grist, destroyed the Ford in a shocking shunt.

Two days later, Burns was McRae's equal. Britain had two world champions. The Englishman's success brought more acceptance from Colin, but, even as the pair mellowed in the coming two years, neither was prepared to accept the other as their better.

The Battle of the Brits rivalry spread across the world, exposing some maginative spellings.

Head-to-head showdown at Rally Australia's floodlit Langley Park superspecial stage.

McRae

2001

Colin was revitalised and ready to hit the ground running in 2001. The Focus RS WRC 01, complete with Pirelli instead of Michelin tyres, had further evolved and looked like a car ready to be crowned. One of the changes for the 2001 season was the use of a fly-by-wire throttle, offering instant response from the right foot.

Unfortunately, it was this part which failed while McRae was engaged in a tooth and nail fight for a first Monte win. The Scot found little more favour in Sweden, where he dropped the car into a third-stage ditch and spent the next five minutes frantically digging it out. The only upside to Sweden had been the conditions, which were absolutely perfect for the WRC's winter rally.

The conditions on the next round in Portugal couldn't have been worse. Heavy rain doesn't come close. Not even heavy rain on top of heavy rain comes close. A blown engine compounded McRae's agony while fuel pump failure in Spain a fortnight later completed his agony.

Four rounds in and Colin had scored nothing. Not a point. Fortunately for him, nobody was running away with the title; three different drivers had taken victory from those first four rounds.

But only one driver would take victory for the next three. In a staggering turnaround in fortunes, Colin won successive events in Argentina, Cyprus and Greece to go from nowhere to the joint lead of the championship.

And he'd done so by demonstrating just what an accomplished driver he had become. In South America, he was on a mission. He was flat-out right from the start and never looked like losing a rally he led from the opening test to the last.

Cyprus and the Acropolis called for an entirely different approach, but again, Colin mastered the tactics and the need for keeping a little in reserve in the rocks.

Hat-trick done, a fourth win went out of the window with steering failure on the Safari, but a solid third and second in Finland and New Zealand respectively kept McRae right at the sharp end. The next two asphalt rounds in Sanremo and Corsica did Colin no favours and brought him no points. The lack of pace was partly due to his own car/tyre combination and partly down to French asphalt specialists – Gilles Panizzi took a Peugeot win in Italy, while Jesus Puras bagged the big points in Ajaccio for Citroën. The championship was barely affected, leaving McRae and Mäkinen tied at the top as they went Down Under.

For the first time, and in an effort to stop the kind of tactical approach which had blighted the mid-season gravel rallies, Rally Australia introduced a system allowing the top 15 drivers to select their positions on the road. Colin was deemed to be late arriving at the selection meeting for day two and was forced to run first on the road. Driving as the sacrificial road-sweeping lamb, he turned in a solid performance to take fifth, a result which gave him a single-point advantage over Mäkinen ahead of a showdown in Cardiff.

Four drivers arrived at Rally GB with a chance of the championship. Beyond Colin and Tommi, Richard Burns was just two points behind, while Carlos was the outside bet, seven down.

This was Colin's moment. And he was ready for it. He blasted his way through St Gwynno and into the lead. But it didn't last long. Driving at a furious pace, he mis-heard a call in Rhondda and sent his Ford spiraling into a monstrous crash. He and Nicky Grist emerged unscathed.

But their car and the title hopes lay in tatters at the side of the road.

## Monte Carlo Rally

January 18–20, 2001
Ford Focus RS WRC 01
Retired

There were very few world championship rallies that Colin never won. Monte Carlo was one of them and 2001 was our best chance. We were leading on the last day, but on the famous Col de Turini stage we ran into problems. We came into an icy hairpin with everything working as normal, but the car half spun when Colin had no throttle response. For 2001, Ford's [technical director] Christian Loriaux had designed a new fly-by-wire electronic throttle system and it had failed. Colin switched the car off, rebooted the system and we got going again. But he was furious – Tommi Mäkinen had passed us on the stage. The throttle failed again after the Col so we had to stop and fit the back-up system, which was a proper cable, which had to be physically connected.

While Colin was fixing this throttle on the stage, swearing like mad at me to "…get the fucking tools…", the television helicopter arrived to capture the drama. Colin was so angry, he slammed down the bonnet and started kicking it so that he could get the locking-pin back in. All this was being captured on film from the helicopter

buzzing overhead. So the next thing was Colin throwing the spanners in frustration.

We reached the end of the Turini and Colin got on the radio to Malcolm, again cursing and fuming like mad. Malcolm told Colin that he must get through the next stage and bring the car back to Monte Carlo at all costs. Colin pointed out that the throttle fix wasn't working properly so the Ford technicians explained how he could adjust the throttle to get it working again. So I got the tools out again and Colin said to me: "Where's the fucking 10-mil spanner?" To which I had to tell him: "You fucking threw it off the side of the mountain, you twat. We haven't got one!"

The sad thing was he'd driven brilliantly and that Monte Carlo victory was gone through no fault of his own.

*Nicky Grist*

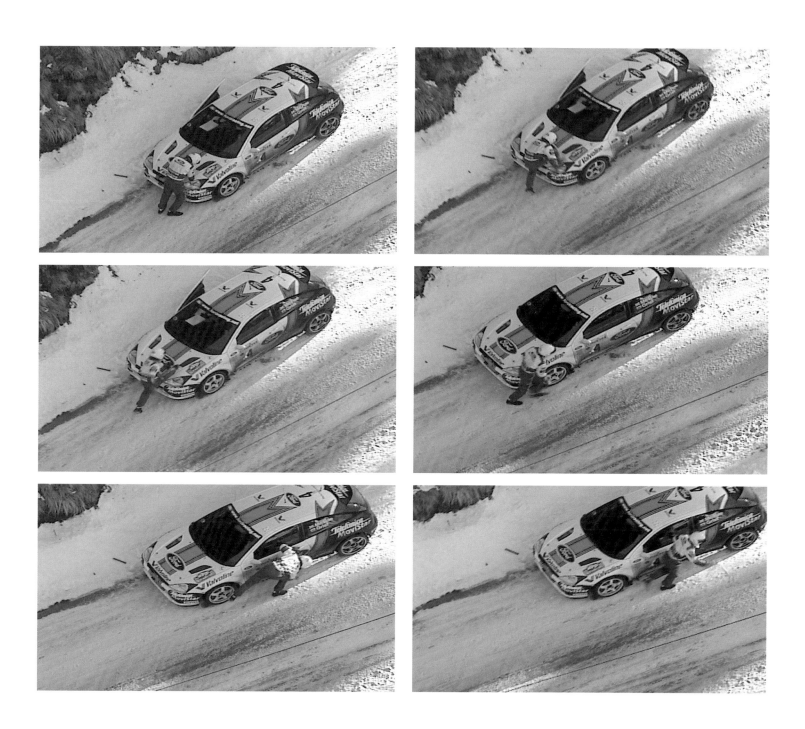

Cyprus Rally 2001

## Acropolis Rally
June 15–17, 2001
Ford Focus RS WRC 01
First

Everybody knows how fast and wild Colin was on sprint events but he was one of the cleverest drivers on the difficult events where you have to know how hard to push the car on certain terrain. Colin had a better mechanical understanding of a car than any other driver we've ever worked with.

*Malcolm Wilson*

Phil Short's split times weren't always welcome. Here Shorty shows Carlos Sainz he's 21 seconds down on his team-mate.

## Rally Finland

August 24–26, 2001
Ford Focus RS WRC 01
Third

I was responsible for the in-stage split-time signalling we used at Ford to try and manipulate road position. In those days it was quite an unsophisticated affair and I would say Colin was not a fan of it. He was more of a seat-of-the-pants driver who would drive as fast he thought he needed to, not what a split-time suggested.

*Phil Short*

Even the English Royal family was well aware of the perceived rivalry between Britain's two best rally drivers.

## » Memories of Colin

Colin wasn't a great one for waiting in airports, but he had a great story from when he was in the lounge at Edinburgh airport one time and somebody came over to him and said: "You are Colin McRae aren't you?" and Colin said yes, but a bit warily. This big burly fellow said: "Would you mind? There's somebody over here who would like to speak to you?" He was a bit reticent, he'd just got himself a coffee and was probably in having one of his don't disturb me moments. But the man was quite persistent and Colin said: "Aye, OK…"

So he walked over and it was Prince William.

Obviously, Prince William knew something of the sport because, in his exact words, he said to Colin: "Is it right that you and Burnsie don't get on?"

Colin was quite taken aback at the way he said Burnsie and not Richard Burns.

*Margaret McRae*

Inside the image, on the start list:

OFFICIAL START LIST

| POSITION | DRIVER |
|----------|--------|
| 1 | |
| 2 | |
| 3 | |
| 4 | |
| 5 | |
| 6 | |
| 7 | |
| 8 | 4 C MCRAE |
| 9 | 16 H ROVANPERA |
| 10 | 2 D AURIOL |
| 11 | 5 R BURNS |
| 12 | 1 M GRONHOLM |
| 13 | |
| 14 | |

# Rally Australia
November 1–4, 2001
Ford Focus RS WRC 01
Fifth

*In order to combat a tactical approach to drivers trying to avoid running first on the road, the Rally Australia organisers introduced a system where the top 15 drivers – in championship order – selected their position on the road for the opening day. Priority for selecting day two road position would be given to the rally leader after day one, the remaining 14 picks going in descending overall position. The drivers were all required to arrive at Langley Park for the selection process at an allotted time. Colin McRae was deemed to have arrived late and was, in accordance with the regulations, 15th and last to select his place on the road.*

The ballot [selection] and its timing wasn't kept a secret from the team managers. Somebody within the Ford camp dropped their ball and let Colin wander off and do his own thing. I was in an incredibly awkward position when Colin turned up late and tried to walk up on stage. I had no choice but to grab him and say: "Sorry Colin, you haven't made it on time and you've forfeited your right, so you get the last choice." I knew what this meant for Colin, but I also knew that, for Rally Australia to have any credibility, I had to apply the rules, irrespective of who it was or what the circumstances were. It had enormous ramifications and quite possibly cost him the championship. I don't put it down as Colin's fault, I think it is the team's responsibility and as much as I like Nicky Grist, it is also the co-driver's responsibility to manage the driver.

*Garry Connelly, Rally Australia Clerk of The Course*

Subaru's briefing document for Australia in 2001 stressed that the road position selection ballot was THE MOST important thing of the whole rally. At the team briefing before the event it was stressed again; the night before start it was stressed again and when we came into the service regroup a few hours before the ballot we were told: "Remember, you HAVE to be back here at such and such a time and the co-drivers are responsible for making sure the drivers arrive."

I remember very well everybody being gathered down at the stage and as the clock ticked past the allocated hour, there was no sign of Colin McRae. Garry Connelly was faced with the difficult task of deciding what to do as drivers, co-drivers and team managers all started looking at their watches. As Gary was nervously looking around deciding what to do, Colin appeared in the distance sauntering along towards the stage, completely in his own time, not even running. It was almost as if he was trying to make a statement, that he would do it his way. The way I saw it, Colin liked to do things his way. This wasn't necessarily a disregard for rules, but if things didn't go his way, then, for him, the rules were stupid.

*Robert Reid*

Garry Connelly wouldn't have known the build up as to why Colin was late, the fact was the drivers had to be there at such-and-such a time and Colin wasn't there at the time he was supposed to be. Because he wasn't on time he lost his right to choose his start position and we were forced to run as the first car on the road. I did my best to get him there on time, but in the end Colin blamed it on me, which he was always going to do. Sometimes, as a co-driver, you have to take things on the chin. I'm one to put things out in the open whereas Colin's natural shyness would let things fester up inside him and this would make matters worse. Although Colin was very vocal on what he thought and what he did, he hated confrontation. Our relationship was getting a bit rocky, so before Rally GB Malcolm Wilson got us together up at his place to literally bang our heads together and sort things out.

*Nicky Grist*

Bunnings and the ball bearings (inset). Western Australia's famous red gravel made the right place on the road a vital component to success down under. Traction wasn't a problem at this point for Colin...

This is what comes of cutting a "Don't cut". McRae's title hopes ended with a major shunt in Rhondda. Burns went on to take the title.

## Rally of Great Britain

November 23–25, 2001
Ford Focus RS WRC 01
Retired

Going into the final round of the championship we were one point ahead of Tommi Mäkinen and two points ahead of Richard Burns. We weren't so bothered about Tommi because we knew he wasn't that fast in GB, but we knew trouble was going to come from Richard. Before the rally we spoke about what to do and we decided all we needed was just to keep in front of Richard. On Thursday we did the evening super-special near Cardiff Docks and were leading the rally before the real stuff started in the Welsh forests on Friday morning. The day began with bright sunshine and at 0730 we started the first stage in St Gwynno with the intention of going flat-out and catching Richard asleep. Colin drove progressively faster and faster, he absolutely drove his heart out on that stage and we beat Richard by about five seconds. In the next stage Marcus Grönholm, Didier Auriol and Richard all beat us, but it was really close. Before the third stage of the day, I told Colin that we didn't need to be going this hard, but he wasn't having any of it. He wanted to have a buffer of

30 seconds to Richard in case we got a puncture or something. We went into the Rhondda stage and we were on a real mission. The pacenotes were coming out like machine gun fire. We had: "Five-right-plus and six-left-minus over crest, cut," all coming out in one breath and once Colin heard the word 'cut' he was in too far on the right-hander. It was a corner you couldn't cut because of tree stumps and we were launched into the air, rolling in a corkscrew trajectory. The car was destroyed and our championship was effectively gone. Again it was another case of Colin's determination to win, when all it needed was a balanced, calm approach.

Colin was gutted. I couldn't get a word out of him after that. We didn't speak for days.

*Nicky Grist*

Richard and I knew that Colin would want a 30-second lead over us, because it was always his tactic to open up a gap and defend it. He probably thought it was his clever secret, but it was common knowledge that that was the way he always approached the rally. If you let McRae get 30 seconds on you, you were knackered so you always had to be on the ball first thing in the morning. We knew that we had to try and not let him open up a gap to us and that's what we did. Colin was fastest on the first stage, we matched him on the second, and on the third – the first long stage – that's where he saw his chance to gain some time. I remember seeing a steaming Ford Focus a long way off the road, it could only have been Colin and I thought: "This is going to be a long two and a half days now…"

Who knows what would have ultimately happened if the battle had gone the full distance, I'm sure each party would have been convinced they would have won.

The first person to phone Richard after he won the world championship was Colin, to congratulate us. It was done through gritted teeth to some extent, but it was done. I think Colin had seen through Nicky's anti-Richard 'campaign', which actually had the reverse effect of bringing the two drivers closer together and putting a wedge between Colin and Nicky. The fact is, Colin wanted to win rallies and he had a disproportionate number of second and third places compared to other drivers. In Australia and GB all Colin had to do was finish just behind Richard, but that would have been difficult for him to accept, for him it was all about winning.

*Robert Reid*

As far as I was concerned the mistake in Australia was a driver and co-driver situation, but it was also the first sign of a lack of respect from Colin towards Nicky. We obviously saw the results of their relationship not being 100 per cent right and the price they had to pay cost them the world championship.

The plan for GB was always to keep Richard behind and after Colin was quickest on the first proper stage I spoke to him to check everything was OK. He assured me that things were fine and there were no dramas with the pace they were setting. You have to go on what your drivers say.

Later, after the event, when I looked at the on-board camera footage, I could see that right up to the accident Colin was driving on the ragged edge. It makes you wonder with Nicky sat there, as he had done for five years, what must he have been thinking? If that wasn't drama, God knows what is.

*Malcolm Wilson*

# Burns and McRae
## Jim Bamber's view

I'd known Colin McRae quite well from the early days and because of that we always had a different relationship to the one he had with Richard Burns. I think they got on quite well and I can't help thinking that a lot of the adverse media stuff was stirred up by Nicky and not by Colin, although he was happy to go along with it. In Greece that year they had placed a photocopy of a Jim Bamber cartoon under the windscreen wiper of Richard's car in parc fermé. It showed Richard polishing Colin's shoes and on the next rally Colin appeared with it on his T-shirt. Of course it was Nicky who commissioned Jim to do the cartoon.

*Robert Reid*

I commissioned Jim Bamber to draw a cartoon showing Colin sat in the driver's seat, with a massive right foot on the pedals and his head flipped open, with me holding a magnifying glass, peering in trying to find his brain. The strap-line for the cartoon was: "The driver's got the foot, but the co-driver's got the brains." I had it printed onto T-shirts to sell to co-drivers as a bit fun. When Robert Reid saw it he got really uptight about it, so Colin said: "Right, I'm gonna get one done now." So that's when Bamber's cartoon appeared, taking a snipe at Burnsie, which of course upset Robert even more and that got Burnsie rattled. There was always a continuous wind-up between Robert, Richard, Colin & me. They worked in a very different way to us, they were so very intense about everything, so you didn't have to do very much or even say a lot for them to get wound up. It was always Colin who won the PR war in the UK, especially during the Rally GB build up. When it came to the media, Richard and Robert would go down this very serious route, whilst Colin would just come out with something wild and outrageous that the press loved to latch on to.

*Nicky Grist*

Safari Rally 2001, McRae shows off his new T-shirt, just to wind up Burnsie.

McRae

2002

2002

1968-1984 1985-1986 1987-1990 1991 1992 1993 1994 1995 1996 1997 1998 1999 2000 2001 2002 2003 2004 2005 2006 2007

TopGear

MINTEX

Ford

Excel RACING

67

COLIN McRae

MIRA    MINTEX

The 2002 was season about hits and misses, with an abundance of pain and frustration suffered along the way. In Corsica the pain was physical when, for the second time in three years, Colin's rally ended prematurely with a trip to Ajaccio's main hospital. On this occasion a side impact against a tree bent both the roll cage and steering column to such an extent that his hand was trapped in between the deformed metalwork. The damage to his little finger was severe enough to cast serious doubts over his participation on the next event.

With typical McRae bravado, Colin laughed off such concerns, talking instead of amputation to speed his return to the cockpit. To retain his full complement of pinkies, Ford moved the gear-shift to the left of the steering column, allowing him to use his right hand on the wheel. The heavily bandaged left hand operated the gears.

Eleven days after the Corsica accident Colin drove over the start ramp in Catalunya.

Much of the season's frustration came from an ageing Focus, hamstrung by Ford's decision to stick with Pirelli tyres. Michelin had upped their game to the extent that most observers reckoned the French rubber superior to the Italian's, on all but the roughest terrains. It was, therefore, no surprise that Colin's two wins came on the Acropolis and Safari rallies – events requiring a measured approach and a fair amount of mechanical sympathy for success.

A third win looked on the cards in Cyprus, until the Scot rolled twice – on separate stages – on the final day, relegating his Focus from first to sixth place. Along with the loss of a potential win, came the wrath of team boss Malcolm Wilson.

Tensions between McRae and Grist were also growing. During Rallye Deutschland in August they transgressed from private to public when, to a TV reporter, Colin referred to Nicky as "The Welsh Wizard," after an error from the right-hand side of the car resulted in road penalties.

A rally-ending accident in New Zealand did the same to the McRae-Grist partnership. McRae felt the shunt was due to a miscommunication and by the time he left Auckland, the 1995 world champion had agreed to be re-united with the man who had shared that glory. Ringer would ride alongside Colin again for the season's final two rallies.

The marriage between Ford and McRae was also set for divorce. The following year would be a transition year for the Blue Oval. While a new car was being developed, there would be no budget for expensive, high-profile drivers. Citroën was a team on the up and Colin had seen his biggest rival Richard Burns make a successful move to Peugeot at the end of 2001, so it was a straightforward decision to say "oui" when Guy Fréquelin came knocking with a contract with Citroën for 2003. Allez McRae!

# Monte Carlo Rally

January 18–20, 2002
Ford Focus RS WRC 02
Fourth

Colin invited me to join him, Alister and some friends for dinner at a posh Monte Carlo restaurant. Colin knew a lot of people, but he was always faithful to his gang and he liked to have fun with them. At dinner, one of his mates left the table to go to the toilet, just as his food arrived – tagliatelle with lobster. The next thing, Colin was under the table, taking his socks off; he buried them in his mate's tagliatelle. The mate came back and Colin didn't say a word, while everybody else was just pissing themselves. It took about five minutes before this mate realised that Colin's dirty socks were in his lobster pasta. From the restaurant the next stop was Stars and Bars in the harbour. I was already hammered. When I thought it was time to leave I tried to sneak out, but Colin shouted: "Where are you going? Are you trying to escape? If you're with the gang, you stay with the gang!"

*Christian Loriaux*

# Tour de Corse

March 8–10, 2002
Ford Focus RS WRC 02
Retired

When we slid off there was quite a solid thump against a tree on Colin's side of the car. For me it wasn't too bad and when I asked Colin if he was all right, he said he was OK so I pressed the 'OK' button on the emergency console and got out to slow the next car down. When I went back to our car, Colin still hadn't got out and I could see the blood had drained out of face and he was looking quite grey. I asked him again if he was alright. This time he said: "No, not really."

The impact with the tree was right on the forward edge of his door and this had pushed the A-pillar inwards, crushing his hand against the steering wheel. He was also trapped because another piece of the roll-cage had bent over the top of the bucket seat. He was in agony from his broken finger and he also had to nearly dislocate his hip to get out of the seat. He looked really dodgy, so I decided to open up the emergency console and change the transmission signal to 'SOS'. The medical helicopter came, landed on the stage and took Colin off to hospital. He would be doing the next rally, in 10 days time, with a broken finger.

*Nicky Grist*

A McRae Focus made contact with a Corsican tree for the second time in three years.

Ten days after smashing his little finger in Corsica, McRae drove a modified Focus (gearshift moved to the left-hand side of the steering column) in Sanremo. And, yes, Colin, that makes two shunts in Corsica…

## Cyprus Rally

April 19–21, 2002
Ford Focus RS WRC 02
Sixth

Leading on the final day we had the rally in the bag, then Colin rolled.
I thought: "Fine, OK, not what we want but he's still in second place",
so I could accept that. Then he goes and rolls again, I wasn't happy.

*Malcolm Wilson*

Top drivers are very conscious of the lines left by the other cars
through corners. They're constantly looking at and reading these
things to see where the other guys have been. On the last day
in Cyprus, our team-mate Markko Märtin had cut a left-hand
corner, rolled and got going again. When Colin saw Markko's line
disappearing into a small grassy bush, he thought: "I'll have some
of that..." Behind the little bush was a concrete bridge parapet and
when we hit it, we rolled too. We got to service and the mechanics
repaired the car. We had been leading confortably, but we dropped
to second place. However Colin thought he could still go and win the
rally. A classic situation of where he should have tempered things
and accepted second – he just couldn't.

We were then fighting hard for victory with Marcus Grönholm, who
was driving really well that day. On the next stage there was a fifth-
gear corner, which Colin went steaming into in sixth. There was no
way we were going to make it. Whoosh-bing-bang-bosh, we rolled
again. The car stopped on its wheels, Colin set off again in first gear
and I couldn't make any sense of the notes at all. We were going the
wrong way up the road!

*Nicky Grist*

Colin McRae driving his battered Ford on the final day of Cyprus 2002 is a sight I will never forget. I was following McRae from the TV helicopter, photographing him from the air. It was like a scene from the movie *Mad Max* watching Colin throwing his re-profiled Focus through the stage. It made for some awesome pictures.

At the stage end we landed to get shots of Nicky and Colin repairing the car. Colin was quite philosophical about what had happened - not upset at all. The boot wouldn't shut and I took some pictures of him trying to straighten the tailgate by kicking it. Of course this was the picture that was used all over the world. Motorsport News ran it full-page on their cover with the headline: 'McRage!' A bit unfair I thought, Colin knew that he was the one to blame for what had happened, he'd let the team down and was genuinely sorry for that.

*Colin McMaster*

## Acropolis Rally

June 14–16, 2002
Ford Focus RS WRC 02
First

Colin was the king of Acropolis. In 2002, we were team-mates and when I was leading the Acropolis by a minute everybody thought it was because of my road position, except Colin. Colin was really cool about it. It was great feeling as I was the junior driver in the team leading the rally. Except I got a puncture and lost the lead and what would have been my first win.

*Marko Märtin*

# Safari Rally

July 11–14, 2002
Ford Focus RS WRC 02
First

By 2002, Colin had really got into the swing of the Safari and if ever there was a perfect Safari victory, this was it. The rally was held in July and, although this was after the rainy season, there was still quite a possibility of some rain. There was one competitive section, close to the Mau Narok escarpment, that went through a vast agricultural area with lovely flat grain fields. The roads there had been continuously re-graded, so much so that they were often a couple of feet below the level of the fields. If it rained the water would come off the fields and flood the roads, turning them into mud baths. Juha Kankkunen warned us about this, so we made special notes for some specific areas where we could get off the road and drive along the side, if needed. On the rally we came across one of these areas where Colin thought the road was quite rough and he reckoned it would be quicker to drive on the fields anyway, so he did. That was one of the things about the Safari Rally, you had to make the best of what was there.

*Nicky Grist*

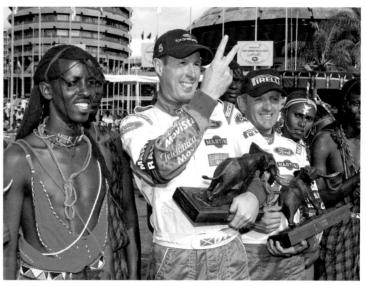

Colin celebrates a Safari win in 2002. But he clearly can't count – that made it three...

The road less travelled. McRae heeded Kankkunen's advice and took to the fields when the going got too rough on the road.

## Rally Finland
August 8–11, 2002
Ford Focus RS WRC 02
Retired

A podium finish looked on the cards for Colin in Finland, before disaster struck, with just two stages left to run. A loose stone pierced a hydraulic fluid line, triggering a fire that would all but destroy the Ford Focus. Colin and Nicky could only sit and watch.

## Deutschland Rally

August 23–25, 2002
Ford Focus RS WRC 02
Fourth

On the first day we checked out of service one minute late, incurring a 10-second penalty. When the television interviewer asked Colin what happened, he said: "You'd better ask the Welsh wizard…"

After this, Colin wouldn't speak to me for a day and half – which when you're sat in a rally car together is not good. We had to do the really dreadful stages in the Baumholder military camp, where we never got into a rhythm and we must have spun two or three times and as a consequence, we lost far more time through driving issues than we did with the lateness penalty. Because I'd lost us 10 seconds it was the end of the world for Colin; what I'd done was criminal. If I had been sat alongside someone like Kankkunen, he would have said: "Don't worry about it."

In 2002, the competition was so close that you couldn't afford to lose any time anywhere. A driver could make a mistake and it would be acceptable, but a co-driver couldn't.

*Nicky Grist*

A stunning scene at the St Wendel street stage. A flash of flame lights up the back of the Focus as the inch-perfect McRae drifts the Ford through the kerb-side apex.

# ASCAR Rockingham Oval Circuit UK

September 14, 2002
Ford Taurus
Sixth

This was a one-off drive which only involved left-hand corners. Colin was invited to drive a 190mph Ford Taurus at the Rockingham Oval circuit in the fledgling ASCAR series, the UK's equivalent to NASCAR racing. The Scot adapted really well and left many of the regular drivers slightly embarrassed when he finished in sixth place. Had it not been for a late puncture, sixth could well have been third.

A rumble at Rockingham. Hundreds of horsepower in a rear-wheel drive car capable of 190mph – what's not to like? McRae quickly mastered the art of turning left.

The car – and McRae and Grist's relationship – were ditched on Whaanga Coast in 2002.

# Rally New Zealand
October 3–6, 2002
Ford Focus RS WRC 02
Retired

Colin misheard the note and we went off the road. We slid down the bank and were out of the rally. It was about three kilometres from the end of the stage and after Colin got out of the car, he just walked off in a huff. I stayed with the car and later went back to the hotel. I received a phone call from Australia from a female reporter for Channel 10 television. She said that she'd been told: "Nicky Grist does not know it yet, but he is not doing Australia. Or the rest of the season."

I hadn't spoken to Colin for two days since the accident, so I rang him up to talk to him about what the journalist had said. I said: "Listen Col, everybody knows about it, except me. We've been through a lot over the years and no matter what you think, I'm really saddened to find out about it like this – from somebody who's not even in this country. I want to see you and I want to see you now to sort this out."

Colin came to my room looking like a little puppy with his tail between his legs. I knew he hated confrontations, so I said to him:

"Whatever decision you've made, that's fair enough. But I thought our relationship was better than this and that you could have at least come to me and told me yourself. Once this comes out in the press there will be a lot of digging around by journalists. I will not be slagging you off and I don't want you to be slagging me off, is that fair enough?" He said: "Yep, that's fair enough."

I was a little bit surprised by his decision, because things between us weren't that bad. But all of a sudden everything was turned on his head because he'd misheard a pacenote and we'd gone off. I think, ultimately, our time rallying together was a very successful and productive one. We worked well together as a team and if only he could have been a little bit more open with me, spoken to me more about problems, then we could have ironed out any issues. It was only during the recce for New Zealand that we were talking about 2003, the contract with Citroën and that I'd be going with him.

*Nicky Grist*

## Sanremo Rally
September 19–22, 2002
Ford Focus RS WRC 02
Eighth

Towards the end of Colin's career the WRC cars were going further and further away from his natural style of driving. I think it was difficult for him to drive them fast because it became all about keeping the car in a straight line. Colin was always very spectacular coming into the corners and his way of setting a car up made him one of the quickest in the old style of rally cars. Another thing with Colin was, the more spectators there were on a corner then the more speed he would give it and the little bit more sideways he would go.

*Nicky Grist*

McRae was a favourite with the team, especially Martin Wilkinson (left) and Christian Loriaux (right).

## Rally of Great Britain

November 14–17, 2002
Ford Focus RS WRC 02
Fifth

If the mechanics at M-Sport could have chosen whose car they would work on, they'd all have preferred it to be Colin's. I'm not sure if this was because he was British and spoke the same language, because it's not like Colin spoke proper English anyway!

Colin had a lot of passion and sheer determination, that's why people loved him. He really would give blood, sweat and tears to try and win a rally. Because the mechanics knew Colin would fight tooth-and-nail to be at the front, then that egged them on to work harder as well, especially when they were under pressure. I have seen guys hurt themselves quite badly trying to get Colin's cars fixed, some horrendous injuries that have never really been caught on camera. One mechanic split the whole of his lip, clean through, from the bottom of his nose down and had to get it stitched up in the service park.

The events that stick out in the mind are the tough ones, like Safari and Acropolis. In Safari I always sat in the front of Ford's spotter helicopter, so I saw first hand Colin drive every inch of the route. I witnessed every single 'moment' he had driving a Ford in Africa. I also saw him trying to fix his cars and how desperate he was to pull his car out of the stage, even when it was broken. Colin's mechanics would try and squeeze that extra two or three percent out of themselves in service, because they knew Colin would be doing the same out on the stages.

*Martin Wilkinson, M-Sport*

# Burns and McRae
## Friends

by Colin McMaster

McRae versus Burns. The 'Battle of the Brits.' That regular and much-hyped story was a fair reflection of the boys in their cars. Less publicised, was their friendship away from the spotlight. I was fortunate to spend downtime with both of them and to see, close-up, their candid relationship. It was both lovely and bizarre.

McRae and Burns were polar opposites in character, yet they totally respected each other. Often they acted like schoolboys in the playground; Colin was very much one of the lads, part of the gang. Whereas the more reserved and cultured Richard liked to hang out with the girls. When they came together socially there was that north-south magnetic effect: they always had a good laugh, but the number one priority for one was to take the piss out of the other.

First and foremost they were rivals and their competitive genes never slept. If Colin enjoyed a good night with a drink or two, he would sometimes test their friendship and telephone Richard at three o'clock in the morning, just to wind him up.

In Kenya, 2001, both Burns and McRae were early retirees, so they went out in Nairobi together. During dinner, Richard said to Colin: "Look at us. We're the luckiest buggers in the world, aren't we? Without rallying, we would be nothing."

It was a big, but realistic, admission. Their friendship grew stronger after Burns joined the WRC Champions' club later that same year. During the winner's press conference, Colin telephoned Richard to offer his congratulations. That meant a lot to Richard. Secretly, though. He would hardly tell a soul about this call.

By 2003, Colin was a settled family man and Richard was the young buck, a slight role reversal from their formative days. They travelled the world, both driving for different French teams, and often they would unite as Brits, socially for dinner.

When their mutual friend, and fellow rally driver, Robbie Head got married in South Africa (April, 2003) Colin, Alison, Richard and Zoe (Richard's girlfriend) shared a house together in Cape Town for the wedding week. The house was open doors and became the social hub for all the overseas wedding guests; every day – and night – they partied together. It was clear to see then that Britain's greatest ever rally drivers had become good mates.

After being diagnosed with a particularly aggressive brain tumour in November 2003, the final two years of Richard's life were difficult in the extreme. Whenever Colin came to visit Richard, it was obvious just how ill at ease he was seeing his old rival unable to walk or talk. The piss taking was gone for good. I can only hypothesise, but for Colin to contemplate a life for Richard without rallying was unfathomable.

The last time Colin ever saw Richard was a flying visit, literally, but also a memorable one. On a beautiful, late-summer day in 2005, Colin arrived at Richard's Berkshire home by helicopter. Sitting outside on his patio, Richard watched Colin land in his garden. The downdraught from the rotor blades caused a huge patio parasol to take off, spiralling high into the air. It landed far away in a heap of mangled canvas and aluminium. Richard thought this was great, by far the most exciting thing that had happened in his life for a long while.

After Richard's death (November 25, 2005), his friends formed the Richard Burns Foundation – a charity aimed at helping those affected by brain and spine injuries. The RBF's first public appearance came at the 2006 Goodwood Festival of Speed, featuring a collection of seven of Richard's rally cars. Colin gave up his time with pleasure to support the RBF and he even drove Richard's Peugeot 206 WRC car up the famous hill.

Nobody needed to ask Colin to do this. He wanted to do it, in memory of his friend.

Richard Burns and Colin McRae pictured in Sanremo 2003. Once bitter rivals, their relationship had mellowed somewhat with the passing of time.

2001 saw the Burns versus McRae rivalry at its peak. Tensions were high at times, however here in New Zealand the pair joke around during a photoshoot for Motoring News magazine.

In December 2002, both McRae and Burns were awarded special honours by the British Racing Drivers' Club at the Autosport Awards dinner.

▶ McRae signs Richard Burns Foundation T-shirts which were auctioned to raise money for charity at the 2005 Goodwood Festival of Speed.

McRae 2003

1968-1984 | 1985-1986 | 1987-1990 | 1991 | 1992 | 1993 | 1994 | 1995 | 1996 | 1997 | 1998 | 1999 | 2000 | 2001 | 2002 | **2003** | 2004 | 2005 | 2006 | 2007

With no more five millions coming from Ford, Colin McRae crossed the Channel to source some more Euros and find himself another great rally car. A rally car that, in time, would become a history-making rally car.

But the Citroën Xsara WRC was not a rally car made for Colin. It was a car made for the next generation. A generation brought up arriving at the apex of a corner with under rather than oversteer. The Xsara WRC was packed full of technology, but to Colin it remained almost as incomprehensible as an all-French discussion of ramp angles.

At the start of the season, everything looked good. Privately, Colin admitted the car was not like anything he'd come across before, but his natural ability to drive around the absence of a perfect set-up was working in his favour. He equaled his best ever result on the Monte with second place – ensuring a one-two-three for Citroën with Sébastien Loeb ahead and Carlos Sainz behind.

In Sweden McRae was quickest of the Xsaras and ended the event as joint championship leader. By round four in New Zealand, cracks were beginning to show and McRae couldn't get comfortable in the car. It took him five stages to get into the top six times, on the next test, he whacked the suspension and was forced into retirement.

The Xsara was burned out in Argentina, suffered electrical issues in Greece, handling issues in Cyprus. The list went on. By mid-season, McRae's already unlikely title tilt had gone and, worse, rumours were persisting that there might be no room for him at Citroën next season. Such talk was fuelled by speculation that the FIA would be announcing that, come 2004, only two drivers – not three – would be scoring for each manufacturer.

By August, Colin had been told: Carlos would be staying, not him. Ironically, August also brought the rally McRae came closest to winning on. A thunderous run through Finland had him troubling second place, before an error from co-driver Derek Ringer cost them a minute. A sixth-gear roll ensued.

And, from then on, McRae was a model of mediocrity. Something he'd never been before. With no seat for the next season, no desire to drive for a second division team and no intention of driving for free, the Scot found himself facing life without the WRC for the first time in his professional career.

Fourth place on Rally GB, a rally he'd been on the verge of utter dominance 10 years earlier summed up the latter part of Colin's time with Citroën. Had he got to grips with the car, had Citroën found somebody on the same wavelength as the superstar, then it could have come good. As it was, it went bad.

Twelve months earlier, McRae had pushed for a year-long deal with Citroën, keen to keep his options open in case he couldn't find his feet with the French.

For the first time since 1990, Colin McRae went into the winter with nothing sorted for the following season.

That wasn't always the case. Towards the end of the year, following the diagnosis of Richard Burns' brain tumor, Subaru offered Colin the chance to return to Prodrive in 2004 alongside Petter Solberg. McRae tested the Subaru in Wales and was ready to sign when budget cuts from Japan forced a radical rethink. In less time than it took to say bank transfer, Colin was out and Mikko Hirvonen was in.

## » Memories of Colin

Colin's driving style was very flowing. I tried to find a combination of his attacking style with the smoothness of Tommi Mäkinen. Colin was a little too sideways and that meant it was easy to hit something. He liked a car that he could play with and going sideways gave him a bit of a safety margin because his pacenotes weren't that good, they were very basic. I once tried to learn his pacenotes, but I couldn't understand anything about them; they were just flat-out for every corner. People say he couldn't drive the later WRC cars, but I think he drove them faster than he had driven anything before. The old fashioned driving style worked in rallying for a long time, but not with the later WRC cars.

At my wedding in 2003 Tommi, Colin and I were in sitting in the sauna, having a beer, an hour before we had to go to the church. That was when Tommi first said he was going to retire at the end of the year and we were all in tears when he told us. After the wedding there were four people left at the bar: Tommi, Colin, my wife Pernilla and me – it was eight o'clock the next morning. We were the last people to leave the party.

*Petter Solberg*

## Monte Carlo Rally

January 24–26, 2003
Citroën Xsara WRC
Second

We started testing the morning after Rally GB and I remember Colin being really impressed with the Citroën Xsara's chassis. We had further tests in Cyprus, Sweden and France all within the first month with our new team. The first event we did in Monte Carlo went very well and we ended up with the three Citroëns on the podium. Second place was Colin's best ever Monte Carlo result and sitting down at dinner after the rally we thought that the year was going to work out well.

*Derek Ringer*

## » Memories of Colin

When drivers like Sébastien Loeb and Markko Märtin arrived
on the scene they understood that, in order to be fast, you
had to drive in a precise, clean style and not sideways at all.
Everybody in the past had always driven sideways but the new
generation realised that the driving styles of Tommi Mäkinen
and Colin McRae were no good for the WRC cars; it was not
the fastest way to go. If you go sideways you lose a lot of
time. If you look at karting, the guy who is sideways is always
last. Rally drivers then began to adopt the same clean driving
techniques from tarmac to gravel, but for Colin and the older
generation, this was difficult. Sometimes when we went testing
with Colin we encouraged him to drive straight and he would
see from the times that it was faster, but it just wasn't right
for him to drive in this new style. After Colin died, that whole
generation of sideways rally drivers died.

*Christian Loriaux*

McRae arrived in Kemer for the inaugural Rally Turkey as joint leader of the championship with Citroën team-mate Sébastien Loeb. He finished fourth on the event.

## Rally Argentina
May 8–11, 2003
Citroën Xsara WRC
Retired

One theory is we damaged the exhaust on a bridge, the heat built up and eventually an oil line caught fire. If we had driven another 400 metres, over the crest of the next hill, then we could have coasted down to a marshal's point with fire extinguishers and the car might have been saved. We didn't know that, so we bailed-out and watched the car totally burn out. At the same time several acres of pampas were set alight and the organisers had to send a plane to water-bomb the countryside. The car was not handling very well before the fire and Colin thought there was possibly a problem with the hydraulics. All the evidence, however, went up in smoke. It was a total loss, a lot of money. But the main thing is we got out OK.

*Derek Ringer*

# Acropolis Rally

June 5–8, 2003
Citroën Xsara WRC
Fouth

Greece was the first rally of the year that we really thought we could win. We had a fast time on the first stage and the car felt good. On the second stage we were waiting at the start control and suddenly all the electrics went dead. It took three or four minutes to fix and we immediately lost 30 seconds in penalties. On the penultimate stage, the fly-by-wire throttle system failed and I had to get out of the car and jam the throttle half-open. We were limping through the stage and, unbeknown to us, we held Petter Solberg up in our dust. He eventually rammed us to get past and afterwards there were a few questions raised that we had held him up deliberately, which wasn't the case.

*Derek Ringer*

When I caught Colin on the stage he didn't move over despite me flashing my lights and beeping the horn like mad. I followed him for a couple of kilometres, losing a lot of time. In the end, I got so pissed-off that I smacked him hard in the back of his car. I think he was pretty scared by that because afterwards he came to me and asked me what the hell was I doing. It cost me a place in the rally, he was sorry to have held me up, but I couldn't really blame him. There wasn't much space in the stage to move over anyway.

*Petter Solberg*

## Deutschland Rally

July 24–27, 2003
Citroën Xsara WRC
Fourth

2003 was a very competitive year. There were six proper teams, most with three drivers which meant there were at least 15 factory drivers on every event, around 10 of whom were perfectly capable of winning. Even though we were only on the podium once, by producing fourths and fifths we were consistently stacking up points which was great because it was so close that year. Because of the scoring system we were theoretically still in with a chance of winning the championship right up until the penultimate round in Spain. This was the game plan Richard Burns had adopted but this wasn't really in Colin's nature, he was used to dominating certain rallies and in 2003 it just wasn't coming together.

We were really quick in Germany to start with, then the sumpguard fell down at the front and the drag it caused slowed us a lot. You couldn't afford to give away a few seconds if you wanted a good result and we had a massive high speed spin in the vineyards. Fortunately we ended up pointing in the right direction in the middle of the road, so we just kept going.

*Derek Ringer*

A grim-faced Ringer rues his mistake on Rally Finland.

# Rally Finland

August 7–10, 2003
Citroën Xsara WRC
Retired

We had done the classic Ouninpohja stage in the morning, which was due to be repeated in the afternoon. It had gone fairly well and we sat in the car at the service-in time control discussing various changes we wanted to make to the pace notes. Although I had marked the right time on the time card, I was at the control a minute before that time and, by mistake, I handed the card to the marshal before the minute ticked over. I looked at the marshal and she looked back at me, and I could tell that there was no way she was going to change it. Checking in early is basically a hanging offence for a co-driver, because the minute penalty you receive is so severe.

I found it incredibly difficult to concentrate in the afternoon, however we set the fastest time on the second run through Ouninpohja, but on the next stage we crashed.

As a co-driver you are not allowed to make mistakes like that and, after the rally, I just said to Colin that I was sorry, I had made the mistake and I had thrown every chance of a good result away. Although he was disappointed, to his credit, Colin accepted my honesty and appreciated that I did not try to put the blame on somebody else. I admired him for that. We went out for dinner that night with our gravel crew of Campbell Roy and Murray Grierson. The boys said to me that if Nicky had made the same mistake, Colin wouldn't have talked to him for a month.

*Derek Ringer*

McRae emerges from the shortened Xsara after rattling the trees in the Moksi stage.

## Sanremo Rally
October 3–5, 2003
Citroën Xsara WRC
Sixth

We never settled down at Citroën, it was such a change of culture.
Colin was used to working with an engineer who would explain
how they were setting up the car to suit his driving. The situation
with Citroën was slightly different, they expected the driver to tell
them how the car felt and then the engineers would go and change
the car and ask for feedback on the changes. Colin preferred to be
more involved with his engineer and that's how it was at Subaru and
Ford, but not Citroën. Although the Xsara was very, very good, it was
set up for a very precise and straight racing driver style, that was
quite different to Colin's natural style. Colin liked to have a bit more
sideways attitude on the car, for changing direction easily. It was
very difficult for Colin to get the engineers to change the car to suit
his own natural style.

*Derek Ringer*

## Catalunya Rally

October 23–26, 2003
Citroën Xsara WRC
Ninth

Colin didn't believe, until he experienced it for himself, just how difficult it was for a non-French driver to work in a French team. Colin found his experience at Citroën really hard. Citroën's engineering was aimed at making the rally car more effective and efficient which required a slightly changed driving style from Colin in order to make it work. I don't believe for one minute that Colin couldn't adapt his driving style, I just don't think he wanted to. Colin always drove sideways and that worked for him during a certain era but when that no longer worked anymore he didn't want to drive in a different way. Possibly it could have been down to his pace notes. When you are not entirely sure which way the road is going, then a little bit of oversteer is the best thing. It takes extremely accurate pace notes to be able to commit to a corner on the limit with a touch of understeer, because if that corner tightens up a bit more than you're expecting then you're in trouble.

*Robert Reid*

# Rally GB 2003
## Behind the scenes photos

Without a drive for 2004, this was looking like Colin's last outing as a works WRC driver. The occasion needed documenting properly. Colin and Citroën granted Colin McMaster unique access to go behind the scenes and photograph the 1995 world champion, candidly. These photos have never been published before.

▲ No time for computer games, not even for Colin McRae Rally. McRae checks the PR schedule on his laptop, prior to the first Rally GB 2003 photoshoot.

▼ Marriott hotel, Cardiff. A 6:00am start on Thursday November 6, 2003. After a shower and a shave it's straight into Citroën racing overalls before breakfast. The rally shakedown, starting at 8:00am, is near Swansea, approximately 80km away.

Colin's gravel crew of Murray Grierson and Campbell Roy go through the rally route together with Colin, over a cup of coffee at the Marriott hotel in Cardiff.

Recce lunch stop. A small camper van acts as the Citroën team's restaurant for McRae, Carlos Sainz, Derek Ringer and Sébastien Loeb.

The sun is shining and it's time for a private phone call, prior to entering the Swansea service park.

Margam Park, 1:45pm Sunday November 9, 2003. After finishing his last rally for Citroën in fourth place, Colin departs the scene with young Johnny McRae on his shoulders.

McRae

2004

1968-1984 | 1985-1986 | 1987-1990 | 1991 | 1992 | 1993 | 1994 | 1995 | 1996 | 1997 | 1998 | 1999 | 2000 | 2001 | 2002 | 2003 | **2004** | 2005 | 2006 | 2007

Over the closed season, Colin McRae admitted time away from the cockpit of a rally car might not be a bad thing. A fresh perspective.

So, how did he see in the New Year? In the cockpit of a rally car. Where he would stay there for the next 18 days. For the past decade, January had meant Monte Carlo, but this year it would mean Morocco, Mauritania and Mali. The change of continent didn't bring a change in fortune. Trading the Monte for Dakar, still resulted in a winless January.

Colin jumped at the chance to join Nissan's two-year cross-country programme, alongside former Subaru team-mate Ari Vatanen. Having won the Safari Rally only two years earlier, success in Africa was nothing new to Colin, so his two stage wins on the marathon event came as no surprise. Unfortunately serious gearbox problems on his new Nissan ruled him out of the overall running. Twentieth

wasn't what Colin came for, but he took an enormous amount of experience away from the event and would come back stronger the following season.

Colin remained with Nissan throughout the season, competing in the UAE and on Baja Portalegre. The Portuguese event at the end of October brought a breakthrough for McRae and team – they won with the 2005-specification Pickup.

Away from the desert, McRae pursued another long-held fascination: Le Mans. He joined Darren Turner and Rickard Rydell in a Care Racing Ferrari 550 GTS to finish ninth overall and third in class on his debut at La Sarthe.

McRae prepares for Dakar with Nissan team-mates Ari Vatanen (left) and Giniel de Villiers (right).

# Dakar Rally

January 1–18, 2004
Nissan Pickup 2004
20th

As it was his first time on the event, Nissan wanted Colin to have a co-driver who had experience of both WRC and Dakar. WRC co-drivers are used to a lot more accuracy in the pace-notes and have a special 'language' which the desert co-drivers have no real experience of. I had done the 2003 Dakar in a Nissan with Ari Vatanen and Colin needed somebody who he could trust, so we decided to team up and go for it.

We did very little testing, so we decided that we should approach Colin's first Dakar with no stress and just go to Africa to develop the car and learn the event. We set some good stage times early on but then we ran into technical problems and we got stranded in the dunes. After that it became even more important to concentrate on just learning the event.

Colin loved being out in the wild. On the days we got stuck we just sat out there in the desert discussing life, kids, WRC and relationships.

*Tina Thörner*

# Le Mans 24 Hours

June 12–13, 2004
Ferrari 550 Maranello
Drivers: Colin McRae, Rickard Rydell and Darren Turner
Ninth overall; third in GT1

I'd known who Colin was, but I'd never met him before Le Mans. What I found was just how normal a guy he was and how easy he was to get on with; we had a lot of fun at the circuit and off the track. Colin wanted to muck-in whenever he could and, because he was a lot taller than me, and Rickard [Rydell] was somewhere in the middle, we had to adapt our seat. In the garage, Colin was the first guy out with the hacksaw to get stuck in to modifying the seat.

Colin was a really open person and it wasn't a case of him saying: "I'm a World Rally Champion, I know everything there is to know about driving a car."

Instead, he accepted this was a new challenge and came to all us for advice. He adapted really well to it. Every situation that was fired at him, he dealt with. I was really surprised when Colin said he thought driving around Le Mans was more physically demanding than driving on a rally.

He wasn't off the pace at all at Le Mans, something like half a second to seven tenths down. I think if he had returned to it in the following years then his pace would have improved a lot.

During the Le Mans week we spent a lot of time away from the track at a châteaux. I found Colin to be a real kind soul, a lot of fun and somebody who I really enjoyed spending time with. He never wanted to be the centre of attention though – just a down-to-earth bloke who was fantastic at what he did. It was a real pleasure to be with him and he helped make 2004 one of my favourite times ever at Le Mans.

*Darren Turner*

UAE Desert Challenge 2004

Baja Portalegre 2004

McRae

**2005**

1968-1984 | 1985-1986 | 1987-1990 | 1991 | 1992 | 1993 | 1994 | 1995 | 1996 | 1997 | 1998 | 1999 | 2000 | 2001 | 2002 | 2003 | 2004 | **2005** | 2006 | 2007

Four days into the year and it looked like the January jinx might be binned. Colin cleared the 654 kilometres between Agadir and Smara six minutes quicker than anybody. For the second time in as many days, he and co-driver Tina Thörner led the Dakar.

Less than 24 hours later and the dream was over. Caught out by a dry riverbed, the Pickup went end over end while virtually flat-out. The crew walked away from what had been a massive accident. Dakar God Stéphane Peterhansel was following the Nissan through that stretch of Morocco and the Frenchman readily admitted, if he'd been running first on the road, he would have had exactly the same accident.

Putting Dakar behind him, Colin was enjoying his second season of freedom from the constraints of the WRC. And he was building himself a Ford Escort Mk II. Predictably, this wasn't just any old Mk II. McRae Motorsport put together the ultimate machine, complete

with a paddle-shift gearbox. The Scottish National Rally in June brought Colin back together with Nicky Grist. But the pair continued where they left off – in retirement. But this time they were smiling. And those smiles widened further when a seemingly fanciful deal was finalised for the pair to join Škoda's factory team for Rally GB. McRae instantly found common ground with the Fabia WRC and, just as quickly, the team fell in love with its Scottish hero.

McRae was seventh in Wales, an event remembered for all the wrong reasons after Michael 'Beef' Park died from injuries sustained when the Peugeot 307 WRC he was sharing with Markko Märtin went off the road in Margam Park.

Colin returned to the Škoda in Australia. And, in Perth, time was wound back. Running second, McRae was in with a shot at a win. Unfortunately a botched clutch change left the Czech team broken-hearted and cost Colin a podium at the very least.

# Dakar Rally

December 31, 2004 – January 16, 2005
Nissan Pickup 2005
Retired

In 2005, we had a new boss in the Nissan team. Gilles Martineau came in and he told Colin that he needed to find a new co-driver with more experience of Dakar than me. He asked Colin to test five different co-drivers, but in the end he said he wanted me to stay.

Gilles said to Colin, "But Colin, this is man's work…"

I was really happy with Colin's reply. It was so cool. He said to him, "Gilles, if you want to, you drive this car to Dakar. But if you want me to drive this car to Dakar, then Tina is coming with me."

That conversation stopped there.

Together we had some knowledge of Dakar, but Colin had such ability behind the wheel. His competence and confidence was much higher than other drivers. And it was this that allowed Colin to drive much closer to the edge than the others – that was his normal level. But, when you are closer to the limit there are fewer margins for things going wrong.

On the day of the crash, we were leading the rally and opening the road for the first time. I remember we had come through some of the most difficult dunes with brilliant navigation and we were looking good. We had three kilometres to the next checkpoint and then it was flat out for 80 kilometres to the finish of the section. We saw the helicopter leave us, which is a bit of an indication that you are out of the worst section. I think maybe we started to relax a little bit.

We were coming through a dune corridor and there was, what looked like a wave in the sand. We hit it, but it was more like concrete than sand. This sent the car up and then we hit another dune, which was really hard, and the suspension couldn't do anything. We went 'head over heels' at 170kph.

Straight away, I thought: "Oh fuck…"

Inside the car in an accident like this it's like slow motion, you feel the belts going loose [because of the g-forces]. And, in a crash like this, you often lose eyesight briefly; it's the brain's way of dealing with it. So after we stopped, I couldn't see. And neither could Colin.

Colin started to panic. He knew we had 300 litres of fuel on board and he really hated the thought of fire. I was hanging above Colin in my belts when I got some eyesight back. When I saw Colin, his nose was smashed and he was bleeding. He still couldn't see.

I told him he had to come out of his belts and feel his way through the screen in front of him. Eventually, we got out. But then Colin was sitting in the desert for 15 minutes before he could see again. This was a long time.

Straight away, he wanted the sat phone to call his family, but this was strapped to the roll cage and we still weren't sure the car wasn't going to go up…

A while later, once he had made his call, he sat there and said to me: "Tina, promise me one thing: promise me you and me are going to win Dakar together."

I promised him straight away that I would.

I was never afraid in the car with Colin.

*Tina Thörner*

Tina Thörner, Ari Vatanen and Colin can't disguise their African ambition…

McRae flies at the Dakar prologue stage in Lisbon.

I remember after the Dakar crash, he phoned me and said: "Would you do me a favour?" I said yes and wondered what was coming. "Can you book me a brain scan?"

I remember thinking to myself, how many wives have their husband asking them to do that? When he got back home, he was sitting at the kitchen table and I was playing with his hair and it was full black and blue, his whole scalp was covered in a massive bruise.

*Alison McRae*

McRae loved his 'state-of-the-art' Escort Mk II.

## Scottish National Rally

June 11, 2005
Ford Escort MKII
Retired

This was the first rally Colin and I did in the Escort. It started in Dumfries. I stayed at Colin's house the night before and the pair of us set off in the morning in a van with the rally car behind on a trailer. I will always remember us driving down the M74 and the look on some guy's face as he passed us and glanced across to see Colin McRae… driving a van… he did a real double take! He probably couldn't believe what he was seeing.

Colin had spent so many years at the sharp of end of the sport that he had decided to do the things he'd always wanted to do. The Escort was something he was passionate about. And, rather than just buying any old Mk II, he took a Group 4 Escort, changed the suspension geometry, fitted a six-speed gearbox with hydraulic paddle change and moved the petrol tank. He made this car better using modern technology.

In the National rally, we were up against both Jimmy and Alister McRae in a pair of Escorts and one of Colin's best friends, Neale Dougan, in a Subaru WRC car. On the first stage in Ae Forest, the paddle-shift was stuck in sixth gear, yet Colin managed to beat Alister and was only one second slower than Neale. We retired from the rally but Colin had shown everybody what real speed was all about, albeit in a rear-wheel drive Escort. It was a lot of fun.

*Nicky Grist*

# Rally of Great Britain
September 15-18, 2005
Škoda Fabia WRC
Seventh

I was speaking with the Škoda team manager and he told me how the works team faced being closed down unless they could get some decent results. I asked him whether or not they would be interested in Colin McRae doing some rallies for them. Colin was really keen and I think he was quite happy to have me back co-driving again. For me, it felt like the justification [that] our relationship was never really that bad after all. Colin started negotiating with Skoda and we ended up with a two-rally deal for GB and Australia.

We did a big test in Scotland and also drove the Border Counties Rally in Scotland as course car. On Rally GB itself, Colin brought the car home seventh, but we didn't have a good time and everything was overshadowed by the disaster which claimed the life of [Michael] 'Beef' [Park].

Colin had spent nearly two years out of the WRC, and we were expecting to be more competitive than we were. It's never that easy and things had moved on a step since the last time Colin drove in the championship.

From Škoda's point of view, things were different. That one WRC event with Colin brought them more media exposure and PR than they'd had in their previous 20 years of rallying. Immediately they realised the value of having somebody like Colin McRae.

The day after the rally Colin came to the charity golf day, I'd organised. He really let his hair down and enjoyed himself. He even ended up terrorising the photographer, chasing him everywhere in a golf buggy. He couldn't hit a golf ball mind you.

*Nicky Grist*

There was no doubting McRae's ability to drive a rally car. And a return to the WRC with Škoda netted seventh on Rally GB. Driving a golf ball was another story…

McRae passes former team-mate Sébastien Loeb's stricken Citroën on a memorable final run at Rally Australia.

# Rally Australia

November 10-13, 2005
Škoda Fabia WRC
Retired

Colin and I had a lot of retirements in our time and, although this one didn't mean anything for a championship, it meant absolutely everything for the Škoda team who were on the verge of their best ever result.

Sébastien Loeb was out after he went off and hit a tree. Marcus Grönholm also retired. But, even despite those two, we were in the mix of things right from the word go. The surface was difficult as always in Australia, but Colin drove superbly well and at the mid-point of the final day we were third, just a few seconds behind Harri Rovanperä. And we were confident of taking him.

Normally, at the 45-minute service at the end of the day, the team would do a routine clutch change. It was standard practice. When the engineer had looked at the clutch wear on our car, he decided it wasn't necessary and elected not to change it. However at the 20-minute midday service on the final day his laptop was telling him that the clutch was worn dangerously thin and now needed changing. Colin and I were really chilled out and didn't notice the big kerfuffle going on in the service area as the mechanics frantically set about trying to change the clutch. Škoda's chief engineer Dietmar Mettrich came and told us what was going on and instructed me to go straight to the time control and wait for Colin there.

Our due time out of service came and went, then slowly but surely the maximum lateness time arrived and I knew that was it: we were out – OTL (Outside Time Limit). The service had gone horribly wrong, our mechanics were not confident enough to do the job in such a high-pressure situation and they messed up the clutch change. First it wouldn't go in, then it fell apart, finally they had to get another one from the spares truck and fit it instead.

When I walked back to the service area I saw all the other mechanics from all the other teams had gathered outside Škoda to give their support. Guys from Subaru, Peugeot, Ford and Mitsubishi were all lined up and they gave a big round of applause when the Škoda guys finally finished the job and got our car started. When they knew it was too late, our mechanics were in tears. I felt so sorry for them, I was virtually crying too. These guys had never been thrust into such a high-pressure situation before and they were just about to get their best result ever, until it was all thrown away because of mistakes.

*Nicky Grist*

Škoda's botched clutch change cost them and McRae the chance of a Perth podium. The other teams watched sympathetically as the drama unfolded in Langley Park.

McRae

2006

C. MCRAE

GO!!!!!!!

TOTAL

BFGoodrich

Sabelt

CITROËN

Greenergy

ONM 804V

TOW

1968-1984  1985-1986  1987-1990  1991  1992  1993  1994  1995  1996  1997  1998  1999  2000  2001  2002  2003  2004  2005  **2006**  2007

Cark Mountain, County Donegal. It's the summer of 2006 and there's a world champion in town. Letterkenny's been jumping for days, but this Saturday morning stage is packed.

And one particular downhill left-hander is particularly busy. The approach is quick, but there's an open right, which blocks the view of the masses on this particular junction. You hear the cars first. The unmistakable sound of a Prodrive-sourced flat-four punches through the morning mist of an Irish summer. Kevin Lynch comes and goes. Undramatic, precise. Mark Higgins arrives in the same vein, but short-shifting his Quattro-sounding Mitsubishi Lancer WRC.

Then the noise, carried longer and louder on an opportune gust of wind. There's no turbo here, this one's about plenty of natural aspiration and even more natural talent. An angry-sounding "Blaaaaaa…" from the motor signals more throttle than might be sensible.

"Here he comes," shouts somebody in the crowd. "The boy's comin'…"

A white Metro 6R4 hoves into view from the right-hander; it's on the edge of running out of grip, but the roar from this side of the road keeps it on the right track.

Colin's here.

McRae flicks the car at the left. A momentary lift of the throttle helps the weight transfer and the Metro starts sliding. Taps wide open, right hand down, a whiff of smoke and four black lines are drawn.

Colin's gone. But he's left his mark.

The silence which follows is eerie; a communal catching of breath.

Then the dash to the car, then the proper dash to the next stage. More of the same, please.

This season was all about Colin and cars he really enjoyed. He raced a 911 in Germany, Monaco and Knockhill; rallied his Mk II and 6R4 and said hello to America.

The world's most powerful nation was largely unfamiliar with McRae. America knew the PlayStation figure; the gaming version of Colin reached the four corners of the globe well before the man himself.

August in Los Angeles put that right.

Driving a gold Subaru Impreza, Colin rolled in the final of the X Games in front of thousands of fans downtown and millions on television. The car was still having its accident when McRae found first and urged it towards the finish line.

He was second. But it didn't matter. In 2006, America found itself a real-time hero.

Colin's final competitive outing of the year would turn out to be his final World Rally Championship event ever. He replaced an injured Sébastien Loeb in a Citroën Xsara WRC on the Rally of Turkey. He retired a car he didn't like first time around late in an event which he never came to terms with.

Beyond the number one on the doors of the Xsara, there was little to reconcile this Colin with the world champion who was getting faster and faster a decade earlier.

# Donegal National Rally

June 16–18, 2006
MG Metro 6R4
First

One thing Colin always wanted to do was rally a 6R4. It was great fun and we were up against some serious Irish guys in proper WRC machinery. Not even Colin McRae could make up the performance difference driving a car with 1985 technology.

There was one point when the car got out of phase on a series of bumps. It snapped sideways and we spun-off backwards past a square junction and down the escape road – it looked like a flash of lightning. A 6R4 body is made of plastic so I thought: "Oh Christ, this is going to be messy…"

We stopped, the car stalled and when I looked at Colin, he looked at me and said: "Fucking hell! How did we get away with that?" We couldn't believe our luck and spent the rest of stage laughing about it.

*Nicky Grist*

Colin always fancied a run in the car his father drove 20 years earlier. Spectacular didn't come close. McRae and the Metro 6R4 were a sight to behold.

The roll that rocked America. McRae's spectacular progress towards an X Games silver medal woke the world's most powerful nation and turned virtual… real.

# X Games

California, USA
August 3-6, 2006
Subaru Impreza
Silver medal

The clothing company *No Fear* put together a budget to sponsor a car in the inaugural X Games rally competition. They contacted Colin and we went over to California, not really knowing what to expect. The only two rally drivers we'd heard of from over there were Travis Pastrana and Ken Block.

There was a day of rallying north of Los Angeles, which was in a park consisting mainly of slow twisty stages, using the organiser's pace notes. It was really quite demanding. We went into the first stage intending just to get a feel of things and to try out the notes. When we got the times through, Travis Pastrana had taken 12 seconds out of us. That was it for Colin – the gauntlet had been thrown down and he was going for it. Travis drove really well and on the slow and twisty stages Colin struggled to take any real time out of his initial lead. At the end of the day we were leading by a couple of tenths of a second.

Day two featured one stage finishing inside the Home Depot Stadium, where they had built loads of jumps. You started outside the stadium on tarmac, and then came into the stadium down a huge ramp onto another jump, closely followed by a hairpin right, then some more corners to the finish. Coming into the stadium Colin wanted to finish in style. We came down the big ramp and on the take off for the jump Colin decided to flick the car sideways so that he would land and be set-up for the hairpin right.

The car took off quite severely, landed on the left-front wheel, popped that tyre off the rim and we rolled over. The car landed on its wheels, by which time Colin already had it in first gear and off we went again to the flying finish. We lost to Travis by only half a second. The whole stadium erupted.

That was the point at which America realised that Colin McRae was not some fictitious PlayStation [computer game] caricature. He was real – because this made National news on two major networks. *No Fear* were bowled over by this, it was brilliant PR for them.

*Nicky Grist*

McRae and his fellow Subaru podium dwellers: Ken Block (right, bronze) and Travis Pastrana (centre, gold).

Just the two of us… McRae and Grist were back for one more WRC ride in Turkey, 2006. It didn't go to plan and they retired with a late alternator failure.

## Rally of Turkey

October 13–15, 2006
Citroën Xsara WRC
Retired

Citroën's Sébastien Loeb had fallen off his mountain bike and broken his shoulder, so they asked Colin to come in and do Turkey for them. We hadn't done a WRC event for almost a year and, once again, we weren't too sure what to expect.

We turned up in Turkey and the weather was horrendous: lots and lots of rain. Back in those days you had to nominate your tyres four weeks before the actual event and because we were standing in for Sébastien, we had to use his tyre choice. He had chosen the hardest of the hard compound tyres possible and because of all the mud lying around we wanted to use a soft tyre, which wasn't available. On the rally Colin struggled to get back on the ultimate pace because of a combination of factors.

Firstly, he was back in the Citroën Xsara again, which he never got on with in 2003. Secondly, it was 11 months since he last drove

competitively in the WRC. And thirdly, he didn't have the right tyres for the bad conditions.

In the end we retired on the last stage with an alternator problem. That was the last WRC event Colin McRae ever did.

Colin was mad keen to get back into WRC, but I think that spending more time at home had made him much more relaxed and he was content with family life. Co-driving for him at that time was much easier too, we got on really well and our relationship was as good as it had been at any time before.

*Nicky Grist*

Eleven years earlier, McRae had walked on water… but in Turkey his final WRC outing would end in disappointment.

McRae

2007

1968-1984  1985-1986  1987-1990  1991  1992  1993  1994  1995  1996  1997  1998  1999  2000  2001  2002  2003  2004  2005  2006  **2007**

Fettling the Mk II Escort for a Manx National race against Phil Collins took some of Colin's early season focus. In the end McRae retired just as he was getting the better of his Herefordshire rival, but not before smiles had been delivered to the spectators and the post-event bar filled with quick corners getting quicker.

A more serious proposition came Colin's way around this time – the chance to get back to Dakar with the X-Raid team. He won the Baja Aragon, driving a BMW X3 in June and relished a return to Africa with Tina Thörner alongside the following January.

Soon after his Spanish off-road win, McRae thrilled the Festival goers by spiraling a Subaru Impreza WRC2006 up Lord March's Goodwood driveway. The sight of the Saltire alongside that one-word rallying dynasty in the rear window meant everything to everybody. And it was accompanied by an exhaust note which could only call Colin.

Unbeknown to the hordes of fans enjoying the sunshine on the Sussex Downs that weekend, a deal was being done. The McRae name would be back on the side of a Subaru full time in 2008. Colin and David Richards were plotting the sport's most exciting comeback of all time.

The first part of that comeback was a proper test in the Subaru World Rally Team's current car. And, on the morning of September 15, Colin was talking to SWRT's David Lapworth about the logistics.

The return was coming. The one more shot at the world championship McRae had hankered after was underway. Happy and full of purpose for the following season, on the afternoon of September 15, Colin, his son Johnny and two family friends climbed aboard the helicopter...

McRae took to the sky in a Subaru during X Games, but couldn't match his friend Block's massive 171-foot leap...

McRae's dreams of an X Games gold were shattered by a second successive roll in LA.

## X Games
California, USA
August 2–5, 2007
Subaru Impreza
Retired

It was Colin McRae's style and attitude that inspired me to do what I do with rally cars. Colin had passion and he put his heart into driving. He liked to have fun in amazing vehicles. When I started developing my own skills, I began to realise that Colin and I had so much in common and shared a love for playing with rally cars in a way besides what they were actually built for.

We became friends and when I sent him the photo of me jumping my rally car 171 feet, he said that if that was for real then he would eat his own driving boots. My reply was: "Get ready to eat those boots!"

In 2007 Colin came back to X Games and we had a lot more fun because we knew each other better. He stayed close by my family and we hung out together for a few days before the event, which would turn out to be his last ever competition. He didn't finish it, however, because he crashed when we went head-to-head inside the stadium.

Having Colin be a part of our team was just a dream come true, something I'll never forget because he was such a hero of mine.

Before he died, Colin telephoned me while I was filming a video at a snowboard park in New Zealand. We talked for a while about what I was doing and he told me he was really looking forward to seeing it. I was really upset when he passed away and I never had the chance to show him the video.

*Ken Block*

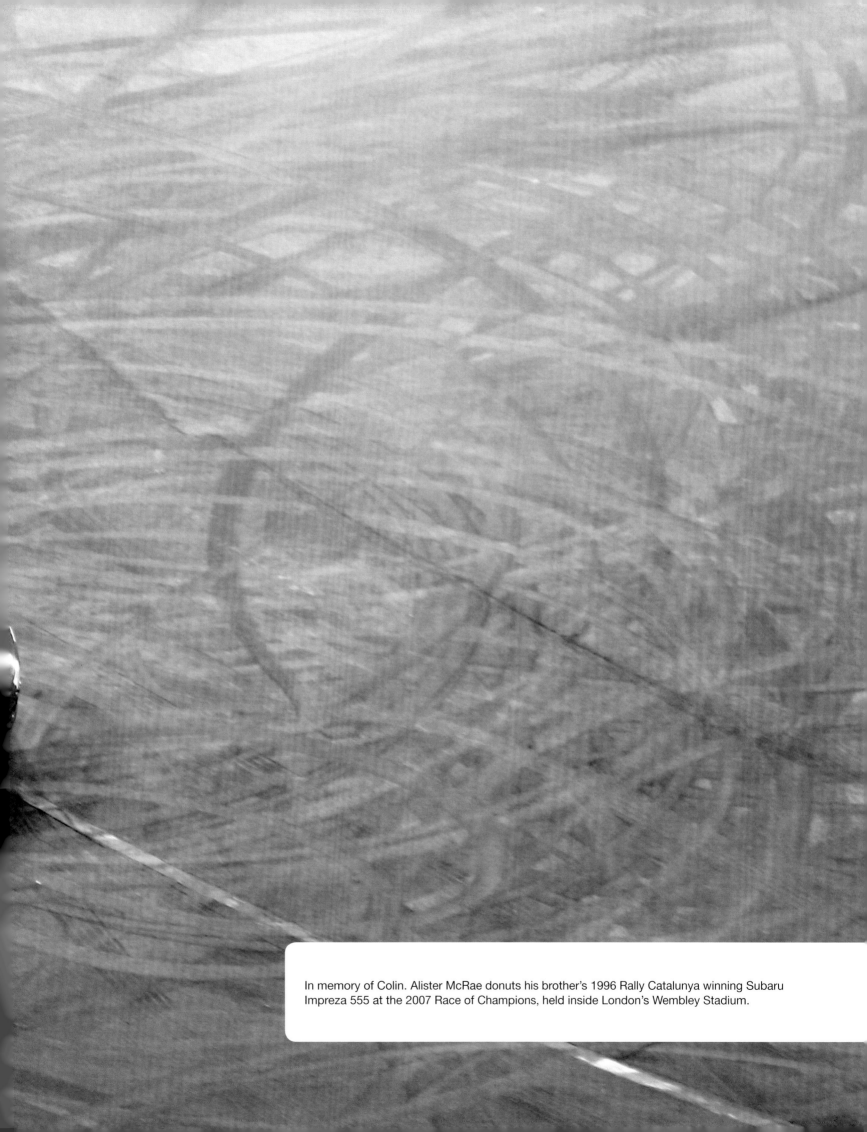

In memory of Colin. Alister McRae donuts his brother's 1996 Rally Catalunya winning Subaru Impreza 555 at the 2007 Race of Champions, held inside London's Wembley Stadium.

# September 15, 2007

## Where were you when...?

Shortly after three o'clock a normal September Saturday afternoon in 2007 became anything but.

Colin McRae's helicopter crashed close to his Lanark home. Colin, his five-year-old son Johnny and family friends Graeme Duncan, 37 and Ben Porcelli, six, all died in the accident. Saturday September 15, 2007 became a day nobody connected with our sport would ever forget.

## Ken Block
Rally Driver and Gymkhana stunt driver

I was at home when I heard. I'd been in New Zealand doing a jump [in a Subaru] at a ski resort and had suffered a compression fracture in my back, but I was back home when I got the call from Derek [Dauncey] my team manager. The last time I spoke to Colin was when I was in New Zealand and I'll never forget that moment.

I was sitting on the porch in a condo alongside Lake Wanaka. One thing Colin and I shared was our love of having fun with the cars. I'd been to his place in Scotland and he'd taken me around Knockhill in the R4, then we talked about doing different things like gymkhana – we had planned to do more stuff together. He called me in New Zealand to see what I was doing and he said he couldn't wait to see the film I was making. For me, that was so cool to have one of my heroes wanting to see what I'd been doing. I had dreamt of being a rally driver all of my life and it was an even bigger dream to compete against one of the true legends of the sport and to become close friends with him was so cool. When he passed away, he left a massive hole and it's tough to think that, actually, that part of my life has gone now.

## David Coulthard

I was sitting in my motorhome at the Belgian Grand Prix when I got a text message from Bob McKenzie – Lee's father – to say that he'd heard there had been an accident close to where Colin's from. And then I sat and watched on the news and started trying to do the usual things which you do when you start to worry, like trying to call his phone. And then, as time passed, it became clear that the accident had involved Colin and other members of the family, and friends.

For anybody who didn't know Colin, this was shocking and for those who were fortunate enough to know him, it was so sad. Colin was such a particular character, an all-round great guy. I was really fond of Colin, we had some great times together with Alison and the children, just having the usual silly, Scottish fun, drinking, talking bollocks and all the rest of it.

I remember the first time he met my better half Karen. Obviously, Karen knew of Colin, but she didn't actually know him. We were in this restaurant when she came back to the table to find Colin with a snail hanging out of his nose. I'm not sure she knew how to take him at first, but she soon saw his great character.

Always a real Scot, though, Colin. That was for sure – I knew this because he roped me into helping him move apartments in Monaco. He refused to pay for a removal firm and hired a van instead; there we were humping cupboards and beds down flights of stairs… and when we'd finished it all, he bought us a pub lunch.

The sport misses Colin dearly, but not as much as his friends and especially his family.

## Dario Franchitti
Three-time Indianapolis 500 winner

I was in Nashville in my office, and had a call from home in Scotland telling me to look at the BBC's website because there's been a helicopter crash in Lanark. The first thing I saw was that it was Jerviswood, and I knew that's where Colin and Alison lived. I thought, 'Oh shit'. I phoned Robert Reid, because I thought maybe he would know more. He said, "I'm just trying to find out, but it's not looking good."

Then the news came through… It was devastating. I was thinking of Colin as a great friend, of Alison losing Jonny as well and the other families involved. There is no any other word for it. Devastating.

I caught a plane back to Scotland for the funeral. I got off the plane in Glasgow, and I switched my UK phone on for the first time in a while, and there were three messages. The usual from friends, "How are you doing? When are you next back?" etc. The third one stopped me in my tracks. "Hi mate, it's Colin…" The weird thing is that he never phoned me before races, even Indy, to say 'hope it's a good race'. This one said: "Get stuck in this weekend mate." You can imagine that rocked me on my feet.

I still have the tribute to Colin on the back of my race helmet. Every time I pull it on that's the last thing I see – Greg (Moore, another friend lost), his helmet and the Colin quote. It's good to have them there, especially if I'm having a bad day; they're like a little gee up, a 'stop messing about and pull your finger out', type thing.

## Nicky Grist

I was in an aeroplane flying to Dublin when the accident happened. When I landed there were a number of phone messages, one of them from [rally journalist] Greg Strange saying: "As soon as you get this, please ring me. It's quite urgent." I rang Greg and he told me that there were reports that Colin's helicopter had crashed with four passengers on board, but they didn't know who they were.

After that I called Neale Dougan [friend and rally driver] who told me the full story. Then all the bad news came. After that my phone just lit up for two days, with interview-after-interview.

## David Lapworth

I was at home and I first got a phone call from Nick Fry, who was in Spa Francorchamps, saying that he had heard a rumour that Colin had had a helicopter accident. When I found out that he had been killed I had some added disbelief because I had only just been speaking to him a few hours earlier. Colin and I had a discussion that very morning about the nitty-gritty of getting him back into our rally car and testing. We were in the process of making his WRC comeback happen with Subaru.

## Jari-Matti Latvala
World Rally Championship driver

I was at home, I don't remember what I was doing, but then I saw on the text news on the television that there had been a helicopter crash with Colin. When I knew he had died, it was unbelievable. Colin was the driver so many people followed, he was the incredible driver. And then when we heard about the other people in the helicopter then it was just so sad. It was the sort of news that you just couldn't believe and didn't want to believe. I remember when I first started in the sport, when Colin was still driving and I would see him on the recce, it was an incredible feeling for me that I was here competing in the same event as him.

## Sébastien Loeb
Nine times World Rally Champion

I was competing on a small rally when I heard about the accident. Guy [Fréquelin] called me to tell me. I was sad, really sad. Colin and I had good times. When he drove for the team it was incredible for me to be in the team with him, he taught me a lot. And we had fun, a lot of fun together. He taught me a lot about having fun too, and sometimes how to play a joke on Carlos! When the accident happened, I was soon to become a dad and I was learning to fly a helicopter as well.

## Christian Loriaux

I was in Corsica, testing. John Steele [M-Sport commercial director] called me and said there had been a helicopter accident in Scotland and that it was Colin. It was a massive shock.

Normally, I have no memory of test roads that I have been to 10 times or more. But I remember this one precisely: the colour of the gravel, the landscape and the shape of the tree stump I sat on. I can see it all so vividly. I spent that night walking around outside the hotel, thinking about all the good times with Colin.

The next morning we moved to a new test location, a long way away. I put down my suitcase next to the boot and went inside the car to press the button that would open it. But I didn't do it. I just sat down and drove off, with my suitcase left on the side of the road. Only at 11 o'clock that night, after a full day of testing, when we arrived at the new hotel, did I realise that my suitcase was not there. I had lost the plot. I drove back across Corsica to get the suitcase, but of course it had gone. I got back to the new hotel at four in the morning, ready for the next day of testing.

My kids had bought me the case as a birthday present. This was its maiden voyage and, because I was going on holiday in France after the test, it was full of my nicest clothes. Among them was a jumper Marcus Grönholm gave me as thanks for providing him with a car to win the first two rallies of 2006. That jumper had more value than anything to me. Like Colin, Marcus is one of the very few drivers that ever offered me something to say thanks.

For sure Colin would have laughed his head off about me losing my case. Like the briefcase incident years before in Corsica, I'll get him back when I get up there!

### Alan McGuinness
Prodrive, 1995 Chief Mechanic on Colin McRae's car

I was in Budapest in Hungary, with a customer who had just taken delivery of two new Prodrive Subaru rally cars. I briefly left the hotel restaurant to take a call from Paul Howarth (SWRT team Manager). Paul told there had been a helicopter accident in Scotland involving Colin, at this point he did not know the circumstances, but he thought it was bad and would call back as soon as he had the facts. I could not believe it could be fatal, after all it was Colin – he had survived lots of accidents.

It was a massive shock, difficult to comprehend; I suddenly felt a long way from home, desperate for more information so the news would actually sink in. I called my wife and broke the news to my family, who told me the story was on TV and Johnny and two others had been killed as well.

The next morning I caught the first flight back to the UK after a long sleepless night, thinking about all the good times with Colin and how awful it must be for his family. I was basically in a daze.

### Kris Meeke
Rally driver

I'd just finished competing on Rally Luxembourg on that Saturday. I was just driving over the ramp when I saw my brother was calling me. I thought he was calling to ask me how the rally had went…

He told me a helicopter had gone down in Lanark, but there wasn't any more news. I was staying in a hotel in Luxembourg that night and sitting there on my own was horrible. My flight was the next morning, but I seriously thought about getting a hire car and just driving home.

I was trying to find out more news all that evening and I eventually got hold of Robbie Head. It was Robbie telling me the news about Johnny that broke me. I was staying at Colin's house when he went from two to four or five. All Johnny ever wanted to do was to be outside on the bike or anything else and I was around there with him.

### Luis Moya
World Rally Championship co-driver

I was at home in Barcelona when I heard, somebody called me, but I didn't believe it. I called Paul Howarth from the Subaru team and asked him. When he said yes, I started to cry. I loved the guy and I still do. He is somewhere up there watching us right now. He was a big friend for me. You know, one time Colin said to me: "Luis, one day, can you co-drive for me?" I said to him, "Colin, I am so proud that you ask me," but I could not do it. I was with Carlos. But Colin was a very, very nice guy and we had some great times and great parties together. And he was a very, very talented driver in the rally and in the test.

## Robert Reid

On the day of the accident, I was in the Lake District, hosting an outdoor training exercise with the MSA Elite programme. We reached the overnight halt and my phone rang, it was David Lapworth with the initial news that Colin's helicopter had gone down. As more details began to emerge, apart from the shock, I faced with the difficult situation of spending the night in a remote bunkhouse with 10 aspiring young rally drivers, for a lot of whom Colin McRae was their hero. We had a few beers that night, in a very sombre mood.

I'd only just spoken to Colin a short time before the crash and everything was perfectly normal; he was out in a field mucking about on quad bikes with some mates. Colin was speaking to Prodrive about driving for Subaru again and he and I had started conversations about me co-driving for him. That's what we had been discussing that day.

## David Richards CBE

My wife, Karen, and I had decided to go across to the Belgium Grand Prix for the weekend and stay at our favourite little hotel, the Roannay, which is just a few hundred yards from the circuit. We set off from home in Warwickshire after lunch, with me flying our helicopter, planning to arrive at the Roannay in time for a relaxed dinner. We needed to stop once en route at a little airfield in the middle of Belgium to refuel. On arrival there I received a text from my friend Ari Vatanen asking if I knew anything about an accident that Colin had been involved in.

We only stopped for about 30 minutes and during that time there were various vague messages as to what had happened but nothing was very clear. However that all changed by the time we arrived at the hotel. By early evening it was very obvious that Colin had been involved in a serious helicopter accident and as time went by so the full extent of the situation unfolded.

It was no longer the relaxed dinner that we had planned but an evening of reflection about all the great times we had enjoyed together; the ups and downs of his years with the Subaru Team, from his most exuberant early days until ultimately becoming World Rally Champion. It was a long reflective dinner and a night during which neither Karen nor I had much sleep.

## Derek Ringer

I was at home in Spain when I received a call from a friend in UK. They said I should watch the BBC news; there had been a helicopter accident. They thought it might involve Colin…

## Marie-Pierre Rossi
Citroën Racing Press & PR Communications

I was watching television when I got a call to say what had happened. We had to prepare some sort of communication, but, to be honest, I was so sad that I couldn't work at all and had to get some help to write this release. It was very hard.

Colin had a strong temper, but he was great and I always enjoyed working with him. Alison once told me that Colin respected me because I stood by my opinions and made him do things he didn't want to do. This is surely one of the greatest compliments I have ever received in my career.

And the ride I had with him in a rally car was another highlight of my career and something I will never forget. After Rally GB in 2003, we went to Lanark for a drive day with Colin. When we'd finished we all went to his local pub and then back to his house for beers. It was fantastic. And so was Colin.

## Carlos Sainz
World Rally Champion 1990 & 1992

I was in the south of Spain in a karting race with my son. Guy Fréquelin called me to tell me the news. It was terrible. I was there at the race, in my helicopter, with my son and it was such a big, big shock. You can imagine that day, when I flew home with my son, I was thinking a lot about all of this terrible story and about Colin and his son and the other people who had died.

### Sir Jackie Stewart
F1 World Champion 1969, 1971 & 1973

I was at home on the day of the accident. My son Mark told me what had happened and the shock was terrible. It wasn't just the shock for Colin, but for everybody who had had been on-board the helicopter – all the families involved.

I knew Colin well and was proud of him as a fellow Scotsman involved at the very top of motorsport. Colin lived his life – and his family life – to the full. But that day, I was just so saddened for everybody involved.

### Martin Wilkinson
Friend and rally engineer

I was with Colin testing the R4 on the Thursday and Friday at Kames in Scotland. In my test notes it says: "Engine gone, need to look for another one." From Kames we went back to the office in Jerviswood and decided we should go and have a look at an engine Colin's pal John Crawford had. Colin was keen to go on Saturday, but I wasn't going to go because I was having a day off with my kids.

That was the trip they made on Saturday. I should have been with Colin in the helicopter.

I was in Carlisle town and I'd just got back to the car when Hamish Kinlock rang me. Hamish, who worked with me on Colin's cars in Lanark, just said: "Ring Colin, because a helicopter has just gone down in Lanark." When I rang Colin's phone it didn't sound right. There was no engaged tone and no answerphone message. I dropped my wife and kids off at home, drove straight to Jerviswood and was there within an hour of the accident.

### Malcolm Wilson OBE

I was at home watching qualifying for the Belgian Grand Prix that weekend. I got a phone call from Martin Wilkinson, he was up there [in Lanark], and he knew what had happened. When he told me, it was complete disbelief; just total disbelief. After everything Colin had done in a car, the accidents he'd come through, nobody expected this. It was hard to comprehend. And such a tragedy.

# Memorial service

## Colin and Johnny: a celebration of their lives

The late September sun beamed down on Lanark High Street as 20,000 voices sang along with Dolly Parton and Kenny Rogers; *Islands in the Stream* was a particular family favourite.

Two weeks and a day after a tragic helicopter accident stunned the town, Scotland and the world came together to celebrate the lives of Johnny and Colin McRae.

Sunday, September 30, 2007, St Nicholas' Parish Church, Lanark.

The great and the good came from all four corners of Colin's world, but when Johnny's teacher talked of the five-year-old being, "a ray of sunshine who brightened up our day," the shocking tragedy of that Saturday was laid bare once again.

Colin's world championship-winning Subaru and a very special Escort Mk II were in Lanark on a day of remembrance.

Former world champion and Colin's team-mate Ari Vatanen with Jimmy McRae on a very emotional day.

Colin will be best remembered in the blue and yellow of Subaru – those colours were well represented in the crowd.

Close to 20,000 fans stood in Lanark High Street to watch the service on a big screen.

Colin's brother Alister makes his way into St Nicholas' Parish Church.

Schoolmate and family friend Robbie Head addressed the crowd in Lanark.

A 1086-strong convoy of Subarus gathered to make a world record-breaking tribute in Imprezas.

# Colin McRae

# Statistics

| Year | Event | Country | Date | Pos. | Entrant/Sponsor | Co-Driver | Car | No. | Reg. No. |
|------|-------|---------|------|------|-----------------|-----------|-----|-----|----------|
| **1985** | | | | | | | | | |
| | Kames Stages | GB | 14/09 | 14th | Coltness Car Club | Gordon Gracie | Talbot Avenger 1600 | | |
| | Kingdom Stages | GB | | | Coltness Car Club | Ann Cavanagh | Talbot Sunbeam Ti | | |
| | Galloway Hills Rally | GB | 8/12 | Ret | McRae Motorsport | Colin Smith | Talbot Sunbeam Ti | | |
| **1986** | | | | | | | | | |
| | Snowman Rally | GB | 15/02 | 27th | McRae Motorsport | Ian Grindrod | Talbot Sunbeam Ti | | YSG980S |
| | Valentine Rally | GB | 14/03 | 15th | McRae Motorsport | Nicky Jack | Talbot Sunbeam Ti | | YSG980S |
| | Granite City Rally | GB | 19/04 | 54th | McRae Motorsport | Nicky Jack | Talbot Sunbeam Ti | | YSG980S |
| | Autofit Stages | GB | 17/05 | 9th | McRae Motorsport | Nicky Jack | Talbot Sunbeam Ti | 35 | YSG980S |
| | Scottish Rally | GB | 7-10/06 | Ret | McRae Motorsport | Nicky Jack | Talbot Sunbeam TI | 65 | YSG980S |
| | Border Rally | GB | 1/08 | 103rd | McRae Motorsport | Nicky Jack | Talbot Sunbeam Ti | | YSG980S |
| | Lindisfarne Rally | GB | 6/09 | Ret | McRae Motorsport | Nicky Jack | Talbot Sunbeam TI | 46 | YSG980S |
| | Kingdom Stages | GB | 13/09 | 18th | McRae Motorsport | Nicky Jack | Talbot Sunbeam TI | 20 | YSG980S |
| | Audi Sport National Rally | GB | 11/10 | | McRae Motorsport | John Meadows | Talbot Sunbeam Ti | 43 | YSG980S |
| **1987** | | | | | | | | | |
| | Swedish Rally | S | 13-14/02 | 36th | British Junior Rally Team | Mike Broad | Vauxhall Nova Sport | 107 | A681DNT |
| | Valentine Rally | GB | 15/03 | 16th | McRae Motorsport/SMT | Derek Ringer | Vauxhall Nova Sport | 19 | A681DNT |
| | Granite City Rally | GB | 4/04 | Ret | McRae Motorsport/SMT | Derek Ringer | Vauxhall Nova Sport | | A681DNT |
| | Scottish Rally | GB | 13-15/06 | Ret | McRae Motorsport/SMT | Derek Ringer | Vauxhall Nova Sport | 30 | A681DNT |
| | Kayel Graphics Rally | GB | 4/07 | | McRae Motorsport/SMT | Derek Ringer | Vauxhall Nova Sport | 32 | A681DNT |
| | Quip Stages | GB | 26/09 | | McRae Motorsport/SMT | Derek Ringer | Vauxhall Nova Sport | 39 | A681DNT |
| | Manx Rally | GB | 10-12/09 | 1st in class | McRae Motorsport/SMT | Derek Ringer | Vauxhall Nova Sport | 28 | A681DNT |
| | Hackle Rally | GB | 17/10 | 11th | McRae Motorsport/SMT | Barry Lochhead | Vauxhall Nova Sport | | A681DNT |
| | Trossachs Rally | GB | 7/11 | Ret | McRae Motorsport/SMT | Derek Ringer | Vauxhall Nova Sport | | A681DNT |
| | RAC Rally | GB | 22-25/11 | Ret | British Junior Rally Team | Derek Ringer | Vauxhall Nova Sport | 85 | A681DNT |
| **1988** | | | | | | | | | |
| | Snowman Rally | GB | 6/02 | 8th | McRae Motorsport/SMT | Derek Ringer | Vauxhall Nova Sport | 16 | A681DNT |
| | Cartel Rally | GB | 20-21/02 | 8th | McRae Motorsport/SMT | Derek Ringer | Vauxhall Nova Sport | 39 | A681DNT |
| | Skip Brown Rally | GB | 12/03 | 3rd in class | Peugeot Talbot Sport | Derek Ringer | Peugeot 309 GTI | 35 | E225HHP |
| | Circuit of Ireland | GB | 2-4/04 | Ret | McRae Motorsport/SMT | Derek Ringer | Vauxhall Nova Sport | | A681DNT |
| | Granite City Rally | GB | 23/04 | 28th | McRae Motorsport/SMT | Derek Ringer | Vauxhall Nova Sport | | A68 DNT |
| | Welsh Rally | GB | 30/04 - 1/05 | 14th | McRae Motorsport/SMT | Derek Ringer | Vauxhall Nova Sport | | A681DNT |
| | Autofit Stages | GB | 14/05 | 2nd | Donald Milne | Derek Ringer | Nissan 240RS | 15 | FXI2376 |
| | Scottish Rally | GB | 11-13/06 | 9th | McRae Motorsport/SMT | Derek Ringer | Vauxhall Nova Sport | 32 | A681DNT |
| | 24 Heures d'Ypres | B | 24-26/06 | Ret | Saxon | Derek Ringer | Vauxhall Nova Sport | | D541UVW |
| | Kayel Graphics Rally | GB | 2/07 | 4th in class | Peugeot Talbot Sport | Derek Ringer | Peugeot 309 GTI | | |
| | Jim Clark Rally | GB | 9/07 | 2nd | McRae Motorsport | Alison Hamilton | Peugeot-Nissan 205 | 36 | |
| | Tweedies Daihatsu Stages | GB | 17/07 | 1st | McRae Motorsport | Alison Hamilton | Nissan 240RS | 13 | FXI2376 |
| | Manx National Rally | GB | 23/07 | Ret | Peugeot Talbot Sport | Derek Ringer | Peugeot 309 GTI | | E225HHP |
| | Ulster Rally | GB | 29-30/07 | 12th | McRae Motorsport/SMT | Derek Ringer | Vauxhall Nova Sport | 23 | A681DNT |
| | Border Rally | GB | 20/08 | 1st | McRae Motorsport | Derek Ringer | Ford Sierra RS Cosworth | 8 | C970MCN |
| | Cumbria Rally | GB | 3/09 | 7th GpN | Peugeot Talbot Sport | Derek Ringer | Peugeot 309 GTI | 20 | E225HHP |
| | Kingdom Stages | GB | 10/09 | 2nd | McRae Motorsport | Derek Ringer | Ford Sierra RS Cosworth | | |
| | Manx Rally | GB | 14-16/09 | 14th | McRae Motorsport/SMT | Derek Ringer | Vauxhall Nova Sport | | A681DNT |
| | Quip Stages | GB | 24/09 | 29th | Peugeot Talbot Sport | Derek Ringer | Peugeot 309 GTI | | E225HHP |
| | Hackle Rally | GB | 1/10 | 1st | McRae Motorsport | Derek Ringer | Ford Sierra RS Cosworth | | |
| | Audi Sport National Rally | GB | 22/10 | Ret | Rallypart | Derek Ringer | Ford Sierra RS Cosworth | 22 | D350SLV |
| | Trossachs Rally | GB | 29/10 | 2nd | McRae Motorsport | Derek Ringer | Ford Sierra RS Cosworth | | |
| | RAC Rally | GB | 20-24/11 | Ret | Peugeot Talbot Sport | Derek Ringer | Peugeot 205 GTI | 111 | E225HHP |

| Year | Event | Country | Date | Pos. | Entrant/Sponsor | Co-Driver | Car | No. | Reg. No. |
|---|---|---|---|---|---|---|---|---|---|
| **1989** | | | | | | | | | |
| | Swedish Rally | S | 6-8/01 | 15th | McRae Motorsport | Derek Ringer | Ford Sierra XR 4x4 | 55 | D513UHK |
| | Mazda Winter Rally | GB | 28/01 | Ret | Rallypart | Derek Ringer | Ford Sierra RS Cosworth | 5 | D350SLV |
| | Cartel Rally | GB | 25-26/02 | Ret | R-E-D | Derek Ringer | Ford Sierra RS Cosworth | 14 | D936UOO |
| | Skip Brown Rally | GB | 11/03 | Ret | Rallypart | Derek Ringer | Ford Sierra RS Cosworth | 9 | D350SLV |
| | Circuit of Ireland | GB | 25-27/03 | 12th | R-E-D | Derek Ringer | Ford Sierra RS Cosworth | 18 | D936UOO |
| | Granite City Rally | GB | 22/04 | Ret | R-E-D | Derek Ringer | Ford Sierra RS Cosworth | | |
| | Welsh Rally | GB | 29-30/04 | Ret | R-E-D | Derek Ringer | Ford Sierra RS Cosworth | 20 | D936UOO |
| | Manx National Rally | GB | 20/05 | 4th | RallyPart | Derek Ringer | Ford Sierra RS Cosworth | 12 | D350SLV |
| | Scottish Rally | GB | 9-12/06 | 6th | R-E-D | Derek Ringer | Ford Sierra RS Cosworth | 16 | F949RTW |
| | Kayel Graphics Rally | GB | 1/07 | Ret | Rallypart | Derek Ringer | Ford Sierra RS Cosworth | 3 | D293GHG |
| | Rally New Zealand | NZ | 15-18/07 | 5th | Gary Smith Motorsport | Derek Ringer | Ford Sierra RS Cosworth | 19 | D933UOO |
| | Ulster Rally | GB | 28-29/07 | Ret | R-E-D | Derek Ringer | Ford Sierra RS Cosworth | 14 | F949RTW |
| | Cumbria Rally | GB | 2/09 | 1st | Gemini/Presspart | Derek Ringer | Ford Sierra RS Cosworth | 4 | Q293GHG |
| | Manx Rally | GB | 13-15/09 | Ret | R-E-D | Derek Ringer | Ford Sierra RS Cosworth | 4 | D541UVW |
| | Trackrod Rally | GB | 23/09 | 1st | Rallypart | Derek Ringer | Ford Sierra RS Cosworth | 3 | D293GHG |
| | Audi Sport National Rally | GB | 21/10 | 3rd | Gemini | Derek Ringer | Ford Sierra RS Cosworth | 6 | D541UVW |
| | RAC Rally | GB | 19-23/11 | Ret | R-E-D | Derek Ringer | Ford Sierra RS Cosworth | 27 | D541UVW |
| **1990** | | | | | | | | | |
| | Cartel Rally | GB | 24-25/02 | 1st | R-E-D | Derek Ringer | Ford Sierra Cosworth | 4 | G97CHK |
| | Circuit of Ireland | GB | 14-16/04 | 3rd | R-E-D | Derek Ringer | Ford Sierra Cosworth | 3 | G97CHK |
| | Welsh Rally | GB | 5-6/05 | Ret | R-E-D | Derek Ringer | Ford Sierra Cosworth | 4 | G97CHK |
| | Scottish Rally | GB | 9-11/06 | 2nd | R-E-D | Derek Ringer | Ford Sierra Cosworth | 4 | D541UVW |
| | 24 Heures d'Ypres | B | 30/06 - 1/07 | 4th | McRae Motorsport | Derek Ringer | Ford Sierra Cosworth | 9 | D541UVW |
| | Ulster Rally | GB | 27-28/07 | 8th | R-E-D | Derek Ringer | Ford Sierra Cosworth | 3 | D372TAR |
| | Manx Rally | GB | 11-14/09 | 3rd | R-E-D | Derek Ringer | Ford Sierra Cosworth | 4 | D541UVW |
| | Hackle Rally | GB | 21/09 | 1st | Hugh Steele | Robert Reid | Ford Escort Mk II Pinto | 4 | NUS877P |
| | Audi Sport National Rally | GB | 20/10 | 2nd | R-E-D | Derek Ringer | Ford Sierra Cosworth 4x4 | 3 | G289DAR |
| | RAC Rally | GB | 25-28/11 | 6th | R-E-D | Derek Ringer | Ford Sierra Cosworth 4x4 | 27 | G289DAR |
| **1991** | | | | | | | | | |
| | Talkland Rally | GB | 22-23/02 | 1st | Rallying Subaru | Derek Ringer | Subaru Legacy RS | 1 | G87VUD |
| | Circuit of Ireland | GB | 30/03 - 1/04 | 1st | Rallying Subaru | Derek Ringer | Subaru Legacy RS | 1 | G87VUD |
| | Welsh Rally | GB | 3-5/05 | Ret | Rallying Subaru | Derek Ringer | Subaru Legacy RS | 1 | G87VUD |
| | Scottish Rally | GB | 31/05 - 1/06 | 1st | Rallying Subaru | Derek Ringer | Subaru Legacy RS | 1 | G87VUD |
| | Ulster Rally | GB | 26-27/06 | Ret | Rallying Subaru | Derek Ringer | Subaru Legacy RS | 1 | H187GUD |
| | Snetterton | GB | | 8th | TVR Tuscan | / | TVR Tuscan | | / |
| | Manx Rally | GB | 10-13/09 | 1st | Rallying Subaru | Derek Ringer | Subaru Legacy RS | 6 | H187GUD |
| | Trackrod/Barkston Rally | GB | | 1st | Rallying Subaru | Graham Scott | Subaru Legacy RS | | |
| | Audi Sport National Rally | GB | 19/10 | 3rd | Rallying Subaru | Derek Ringer | Subaru Legacy RS | 2 | G87VUD |
| | RAC Rally | GB | 24-27/11 | Ret | Rothmans Subaru RT | Derek Ringer | Subaru Legacy RS | 21 | H187GUD |
| **1992** | | | | | | | | | |
| | Arctic Rally | SF | 24-25/01 | | Subaru RT Europe | Derek Ringer | Subaru Legacy RS | | |
| | Swedish Rally | S | 13-16/02 | 2nd | Subaru RT Europe | Derek Ringer | Subaru Legacy RS | 7 | H641JBW |
| | Vauxhall Sport Rally | GB | 21/03 | 1st | Rothmans Subaru RT | Derek Ringer | Subaru Legacy RS | 1 | J314PWL |
| | Pirelli International Rally | GB | 4/04 | 1st | Rothmans Subaru RT | Derek Ringer | Subaru Legacy RS | 1 | J314PWL |
| | Acropolis Rally | GR | 31/05 - 3/06 | 4th | Subaru RT Europe | Derek Ringer | Subaru Legacy RS | 9 | J175SFC |
| | Perth Scottish Rally | GB | 13-15/06 | 1st | Rothmans Subaru RT | Derek Ringer | Subaru Legacy RS | 1 | J314PWL |
| | Rally New Zealand | NZ | 25-28/06 | Ret | Subaru RT Europe | Derek Ringer | Subaru Legacy RS | 4 | J140PWL |
| | BTCC - Knockhill Race 1 | GB | 26/07 | 8th | M Team Mobil | / | BMW 318is | 50 | / |
| | BTCC - Knockhill Race 2 | GB | 26/07 | DSQ | M Team Mobil | / | BMW 318is | 50 | / |
| | Elbow Ulster Rally | GB | 31/07 - 1/08 | 1st | Rothmans Subaru RT | Derek Ringer | Subaru Legacy RS | 1 | J314PWL |
| | Rally Finland | SF | 27-30/08 | 8th | Subaru RT Europe | Derek Ringer | Subaru Legacy RS | 9 | J175SFC |
| | Manx Rally | GB | 9-11/09 | 1st | Rothmans Subaru RT | Derek Ringer | Subaru Legacy RS | 1 | J314PWL |
| | Elonex Rally | GB | 24-25/10 | 1st | Rothmans Subaru RT | Derek Ringer | Subaru Legacy RS | 1 | J314PWL |
| | RAC Rally | GB | 22-25/11 | 6th | Rothmans Subaru RT | Derek Ringer | Subaru Legacy RS | 4 | K282TFD |
| **1993** | | | | | | | | | |
| | Swedish Rally | S | 12-14/02 | 3rd | 555 Subaru World RT | Derek Ringer | Subaru Legacy RS | 2 | K555STE |
| | Rally of Portugal | P | 3-6/03 | 7th | 555 Subaru World RT | Derek Ringer | Subaru Legacy RS | 4 | J555STE |
| | Safari Rally | EAK | 8-12/04 | Ret | Subaru M.S.G./N.Koseki | Derek Ringer | Subaru Vivio 4WD Super KK | 6 | GM52MU123 |
| | Tour de Corse | F | 2-4/05 | 5th | 555 Subaru World RT | Derek Ringer | Subaru Legacy RS | 8 | K282TFD |
| | Acropolis Rally | GR | 30/05 - 1/06 | Ret | 555 Subaru World RT | Derek Ringer | Subaru Legacy RS | 5 | K555PRO |
| | Rally New Zealand | NZ | 5-8/08 | 1st | 555 Subaru World RT | Derek Ringer | Subaru Legacy RS | 7 | K555STE |
| | Rally of Malaysia APRC | MAL | 21-23/08 | 1st | 555 Subaru World RT | Derek Ringer | Subaru Legacy RS | 2 | K555SRT |
| | Rally Australia | AUS | 18-21/09 | 6th | 555 Subaru World RT | Derek Ringer | Subaru Legacy RS | 7 | 555MAC |
| | Hong Kong - Beijing Rally | CN | 23-28/10 | 2nd | 555 Subaru World RT | Derek Ringer | Subaru Legacy RS | | |
| | RAC Rally | GB | 21-24/11 | Ret | 555 Subaru World RT | Derek Ringer | Subaru Impreza 555 | 2 | L555BAT |
| **1994** | | | | | | | | | |
| | Monte Carlo Rally | MC | 22-27/01 | 10th | 555 Subaru World RT | Derek Ringer | Subaru Impreza 555 | 7 | L555SRT |
| | Rally of Portugal | P | 1-4/03 | Ret | 555 Subaru World RT | Derek Ringer | Subaru Impreza 555 | 5 | L555BAT |
| | Tour de Corse | F | 5-7/05 | Ret | 555 Subaru World RT | Derek Ringer | Subaru Impreza 555 | 7 | L555BAT |
| | Acropolis Rally | GR | 28/05 - 1/06 | DSQ | 555 Subaru World RT | Derek Ringer | Subaru Impreza 555 | 7 | L555BAT |
| | Rally Argentina | RA | 30/06 - 2/07 | Ret | 555 Subaru World RT | Derek Ringer | Subaru Impreza 555 | 6 | L555BAT |
| | Rally New Zealand | NZ | 29-31/07 | 1st | 555 Subaru World RT | Derek Ringer | Subaru Impreza 555 | 2 | L555BAT |
| | Rally Australia APRC | AUS | 16-19/09 | 1st | 555 Subaru World RT | Derek Ringer | Subaru Impreza 555 | 2 | L555BAT |
| | Sanremo Rally | I | 10-12/10 | 5th | 555 Subaru World RT | Derek Ringer | Subaru Impreza 555 | 4 | L555BAT |
| | RAC Rally | GB | 20-23/11 | 1st | 555 Subaru World RT | Derek Ringer | Subaru Impreza 555 | 4 | L555BAT |

| Year | Event | Country | Date | Pos. | Entrant/Sponsor | Co-Driver | Car | No. | Reg. No. |
|---|---|---|---|---|---|---|---|---|---|
| **1995** | | | | | | | | | |
| | Monte Carlo Rally | MC | 21-26/01 | Ret | 555 Subaru World RT | Derek Ringer | Subaru Impreza 555 | 4 | L555BAT |
| | Swedish Rally | S | 10-12/02 | Ret | 555 Subaru World RT | Derek Ringer | Subaru Impreza 555 | 4 | L555BAT |
| | Rally of Portugal | P | 8-10/03 | 3rd | 555 Subaru World RT | Derek Ringer | Subaru Impreza 555 | 4 | L555BAT |
| | Tour de Corse | F | 3-5/05 | 5th | 555 Subaru World RT | Derek Ringer | Subaru Impreza 555 | 4 | L555BAT |
| | Rally of Indonesia APRC | RI | 7-9/07 | 1st | 555 Subaru World RT | Derek Ringer | Subaru Impreza 555 | 2 | M555SRT |
| | Rally New Zealand | NZ | 27-30/07 | 1st | 555 Subaru World RT | Derek Ringer | Subaru Impreza 555 | 4 | L555BAT |
| | Rally of Malaysia APRC | MAL | 12-14/08 | Ret | 555 Subaru World RT | Derek Ringer | Subaru Impreza 555 | 1 | M555SRT |
| | Rally Australia | AUS | 15-18/09 | 2nd | 555 Subaru World RT | Derek Ringer | Subaru Impreza 555 | 4 | L555BAT |
| | Rally Catalunya | E | 23-25/10 | 2nd | 555 Subaru World RT | Derek Ringer | Subaru Impreza 555 | 4 | L555BAT |
| | RAC Rally | GB | 19-22/11 | 1st | 555 Subaru World RT | Derek Ringer | Subaru Impreza 555 | 4 | L555BAT |
| **1996** | | | | | | | | | |
| | Swedish Rally | S | 9-11/02 | 3rd | 555 Subaru World RT | Derek Ringer | Subaru Impreza 555 | 1 | N1WRC |
| | Rally of Thailand APRC | T | 3-5/03 | 1st | 555 Subaru World RT | Derek Ringer | Subaru Impreza 555 | 5 | N1WRC |
| | Safari Rally | EAK | 5-7/04 | 4th | 555 Subaru World RT | Derek Ringer | Subaru Impreza 555 | 1 | N1WRC |
| | Rally of Indonesia | RI | 10-12/05 | Ret | 555 Subaru World RT | Derek Ringer | Subaru Impreza 555 | 1 | N1WRC |
| | Acropolis Rally | GR | 2-4/06 | 1st | 555 Subaru World RT | Derek Ringer | Subaru Impreza 555 | 1 | N1WRC |
| | Rally Argentina | RA | 4-6/07 | Ret | 555 Subaru World RT | Derek Ringer | Subaru Impreza 555 | 1 | N1WRC |
| | Rally Finland | SF | 23-26/08 | Ret | 555 Subaru World RT | Derek Ringer | Subaru Impreza 555 | 1 | N1WRC |
| | Rally Australia | AUS | 13-16/09 | 4th | 555 Subaru World RT | Derek Ringer | Subaru Impreza 555 | 1 | N1WRC |
| | Sanremo Rally | I | 13-16/10 | 1st | 555 Subaru World RT | Derek Ringer | Subaru Impreza 555 | 1 | N1WRC |
| | Rally Catalunya | E | 4-6/11 | 1st | 555 Subaru World RT | Derek Ringer | Subaru Impreza 555 | 1 | N1WRC |
| **1997** | | | | | | | | | |
| | Monte Carlo Rally | MC | 17-23/01 | Ret | 555 Subaru World RT | Nicky Grist | Subaru Impreza WRC 97 | 3 | P2WRC |
| | Swedish Rally | S | 8-10/02 | 4th | 555 Subaru World RT | Nicky Grist | Subaru Impreza WRC 97 | 3 | P4WRC |
| | Safari Rally | EAK | 1-3/03 | 1st | 555 Subaru World RT | Nicky Grist | Subaru Impreza WRC 97 | 3 | P8WRC |
| | Rally of Portugal | P | 23-26/03 | Ret | 555 Subaru World RT | Nicky Grist | Subaru Impreza WRC 97 | 3 | P4WRC |
| | Rally Catalunya | E | 14-16/04 | 4th | 555 Subaru World RT | Nicky Grist | Subaru Impreza WRC 97 | 3 | P9WRC |
| | Tour de Corse | F | 5-7/05 | 1st | 555 Subaru World RT | Nicky Grist | Subaru Impreza WRC 97 | 3 | P9WRC |
| | Rally Argentina | RA | 22-24/05 | 2nd | 555 Subaru World RT | Nicky Grist | Subaru Impreza WRC 97 | 3 | P8WRC |
| | Acropolis Rally | GR | 8-10/06 | Ret | 555 Subaru World RT | Nicky Grist | Subaru Impreza WRC 97 | 3 | P12WRC |
| | China Rally APRC | CN | 21-23/06 | 1st | 555 Subaru World RT | Nicky Grist | Subaru Impreza WRC 97 | 1 | 001 (CHINA) |
| | Rally New Zealand | NZ | 2-5/08 | Ret | 555 Subaru World RT | Nicky Grist | Subaru Impreza WRC 97 | 3 | P4WRC |
| | Rally Finland | SF | 29-31/08 | Ret | 555 Subaru World RT | Nicky Grist | Subaru Impreza WRC 97 | 3 | P12WRC |
| | Rally of Indonesia | RI | 19-21/09 | Ret | 555 Subaru World RT | Nicky Grist | Subaru Impreza WRC 97 | 3 | P8WRC |
| | Sanremo Rally | I | 12-15/10 | 1st | 555 Subaru World RT | Nicky Grist | Subaru Impreza WRC 97 | 3 | P7WRC |
| | Rally Australia | AUS | 30/10 - 2/11 | 1st | 555 Subaru World RT | Nicky Grist | Subaru Impreza WRC 97 | 3 | R18WRC |
| | RAC Rally | GB | 23-25/11 | 1st | 555 Subaru World RT | Nicky Grist | Subaru Impreza WRC 97 | 3 | P12WRC |
| **1998** | | | | | | | | | |
| | Monte Carlo Rally | MC | 19-21/01 | 3rd | 555 Subaru World RT | Nicky Grist | Subaru Impreza WRC 98 | 3 | P7WRC |
| | Swedish Rally | S | 6-8/02 | Ret | 555 Subaru World RT | Nicky Grist | Subaru Impreza WRC 98 | 3 | R17WRC |
| | Safari Rally | EAK | 28/02 - 2/03 | Ret | 555 Subaru World RT | Nicky Grist | Subaru Impreza WRC 98 | 3 | R7WRC |
| | Rally of Portugal | P | 22-25/03 | 1st | 555 Subaru World RT | Nicky Grist | Subaru Impreza WRC 98 | 3 | R19WRC |
| | Rally Catalunya | E | 20-22/04 | Ret | 555 Subaru World RT | Nicky Grist | Subaru Impreza WRC 98 | 3 | R9WRC |
| | Tour de Corse | F | 4-6/05 | 1st | 555 Subaru World RT | Nicky Grist | Subaru Impreza WRC 98 | 3 | R11WRC |
| | Rally Argentina | RA | 20-23/05 | 5th | 555 Subaru World RT | Nicky Grist | Subaru Impreza WRC 98 | 3 | R9WRC |
| | Acropolis Rally | GR | 7-9/06 | 1st | 555 Subaru World RT | Nicky Grist | Subaru Impreza WRC 98 | 3 | R11WRC |
| | China Rally APRC | CN | 20-22/06 | 1st | 555 Subaru World RT | Nicky Grist | Subaru Impreza WRC 98 | 1 | 1 (CHINA) |
| | Rally New Zealand | NZ | 24-27/07 | 5th | 555 Subaru World RT | Nicky Grist | Subaru Impreza WRC 98 | 3 | R11WRC |
| | Rally Finland | SF | 21-23/08 | Ret | 555 Subaru World RT | Nicky Grist | Subaru Impreza WRC 98 | 3 | R10WRC |
| | Sanremo Rally | I | 13-15/10 | 3rd | 555 Subaru World RT | Nicky Grist | Subaru Impreza WRC 98 | 3 | R14WRC |
| | Rally Australia | AUS | 5-8/11 | 4th | 555 Subaru World RT | Nicky Grist | Subaru Impreza WRC 98 | 3 | R10WRC |
| | Rally of Great Britain | GB | 22-24/11 | Ret | 555 Subaru World RT | Nicky Grist | Subaru Impreza WRC 98 | 3 | R14WRC |
| **1999** | | | | | | | | | |
| | Monte Carlo Rally | MC | 17-21/01 | DSQ | Ford Motor Company | Nicky Grist | Ford Focus WRC | 7 | S7FMC |
| | Swedish Rally | S | 11-14/02 | Ret | Ford Motor Company | Nicky Grist | Ford Focus WRC | 7 | S7FMC |
| | Safari Rally | EAK | 25-28/02 | 1st | Ford Motor Company | Nicky Grist | Ford Focus WRC | 7 | S9FMC |
| | Rally of Portugal | P | 21-24/03 | 1st | Ford Motor Company | Nicky Grist | Ford Focus WRC | 7 | S7FMC |
| | Rally Catalunya | E | 19-24/04 | Ret | Ford Motor Company | Nicky Grist | Ford Focus WRC | 7 | S10FMC |
| | Tour de Corse | F | 7-9/05 | 4th | Ford Motor Company | Nicky Grist | Ford Focus WRC | 7 | S10FMC |
| | Rally Argentina | RA | 22-25/05 | Ret | Ford Motor Company | Nicky Grist | Ford Focus WRC | 7 | S7FMC |
| | Acropolis Rally | GR | 6-9/06 | Ret | Ford Motor Company | Nicky Grist | Ford Focus WRC | 7 | S10FMC |
| | Rally New Zealand | NZ | 15-18/07 | Ret | Ford Motor Company | Nicky Grist | Ford Focus WRC | 7 | S11FMC |
| | Rally Finland | SF | 20-22/08 | Ret | Ford Motor Company | Nicky Grist | Ford Focus WRC | 7 | S12FMC |
| | China Rally | CN | 16-19/09 | Ret | Ford Motor Company | Nicky Grist | Ford Focus WRC | 7 | S10FMC |
| | Sanremo Rally | I | 11-13/10 | Ret | Ford Motor Company | Nicky Grist | Ford Focus WRC | 7 | S14FMC |
| | Rally Australia | AUS | 4-7/11 | Ret | Ford Motor Company | Nicky Grist | Ford Focus WRC | 7 | S11FMC |
| | Rally of Great Britain | GB | 21-23/11 | Ret | Ford Motor Company | Nicky Grist | Ford Focus WRC | 7 | S6FMC |
| **2000** | | | | | | | | | |
| | Monte Carlo Rally | MC | 20-22/01 | Ret | Ford Motor Company | Nicky Grist | Ford Focus RS WRC | 5 | S6FMC |
| | Swedish Rally | S | 10-13/02 | 3rd | Ford Motor Company | Nicky Grist | Ford Focus RS WRC | 5 | V3FMC |
| | Safari Rally | EAK | 25-27/02 | Ret | Ford Motor Company | Nicky Grist | Ford Focus RS WRC | 5 | S14FMC |
| | Rally of Portugal | P | 16-19/03 | Ret | Ford Motor Company | Nicky Grist | Ford Focus RS WRC | 5 | V3FMC |
| | Rally Catalunya | E | 31/03 - 2/04 | 1st | Ford Motor Company | Nicky Grist | Ford Focus RS WRC | 5 | V5FMC |
| | Rally Argentina | RA | 11-14/05 | Ret | Ford Motor Company | Nicky Grist | Ford Focus RS WRC | 5 | V3FMC |
| | Acropolis Rally | GR | 9-11/06 | 1st | Ford Motor Company | Nicky Grist | Ford Focus RS WRC | 5 | V5FMC |
| | Rally New Zealand | NZ | 13-16/07 | 2nd | Ford Motor Company | Nicky Grist | Ford Focus RS WRC | 5 | V3FMC |
| | Rally Finland | SF | 18-20/08 | 2nd | Ford Motor Company | Nicky Grist | Ford Focus RS WRC | 5 | V7FMC |

| Year | Event | Country | Date | Pos. | Entrant/Sponsor | Co-Driver | Car | No. | Reg. No. |
|---|---|---|---|---|---|---|---|---|---|
| | Cyprus Rally | CY | 8-10/09 | 2nd | Ford Motor Company | Nicky Grist | Ford Focus RS WRC | 5 | V5FMC |
| | Tour de Corse | F | 29/09 - 1/10 | Ret | Ford Motor Company | Nicky Grist | Ford Focus RS WRC | 5 | V7FMC |
| | Sanremo Rally | I | 20-22/10 | 6th | Ford Motor Company | Nicky Grist | Ford Focus RS WRC | 5 | V9FMC |
| | Rally Australia | AUS | 9-12/11 | Ret | Ford Motor Company | Nicky Grist | Ford Focus RS WRC | 5 | V3FMC |
| | Rally of Great Britain | GB | 23-26/11 | Ret | Ford Motor Company | Nicky Grist | Ford Focus RS WRC | 5 | V5FMC |
| **2001** | | | | | | | | | |
| | Monte Carlo Rally | MC | 18-20/01 | Ret | Ford Motor Company | Nicky Grist | Ford Focus RS WRC01 | 4 | V9FMC |
| | Swedish Rally | S | 8-11/02 | 9th | Ford Motor Company | Nicky Grist | Ford Focus RS WRC01 | 4 | V6FMC |
| | Rally of Portugal | P | 8-11/03 | Ret | Ford Motor Company | Nicky Grist | Ford Focus RS WRC01 | 4 | X4FMC |
| | Rally Catalunya | E | 23-25/03 | Ret | Ford Motor Company | Nicky Grist | Ford Focus RS WRC01 | 4 | V9FMC |
| | Rally Argentina | RA | 3-6/05 | 1st | Ford Motor Company | Nicky Grist | Ford Focus RS WRC01 | 4 | X5FMC |
| | Cyprus Rally | CY | 1-3/06 | 1st | Ford Motor Company | Nicky Grist | Ford Focus RS WRC01 | 4 | X7FMC |
| | Acropolis Rally | GR | 15-17/06 | 1st | Ford Motor Company | Nicky Grist | Ford Focus RS WRC01 | 4 | Y4FMC |
| | Safari Rally | EAK | 20-22/07 | Ret | Ford Motor Company | Nicky Grist | Ford Focus RS WRC01 | 4 | X5FMC |
| | Rally Finland | SF | 24-26/08 | 3rd | Ford Motor Company | Nicky Grist | Ford Focus RS WRC01 | 4 | X7FMC |
| | Rally New Zealand | NZ | 20-23/09 | 2nd | Ford Motor Company | Nicky Grist | Ford Focus RS WRC01 | 4 | Y4FMC |
| | Sanremo Rally | I | 4-7/10 | 8th | Ford Motor Company | Nicky Grist | Ford Focus RS WRC01 | 4 | Y5FMC |
| | Tour de Corse | F | 19-21/10 | 11th | Ford Motor Company | Nicky Grist | Ford Focus RS WRC01 | 4 | Y129XEV |
| | Rally Australia | AUS | 1-4/11 | 5th | Ford Motor Company | Nicky Grist | Ford Focus RS WRC01 | 4 | X7FMC |
| | Rally of Great Britain | GB | 23-25/11 | Ret | Ford Motor Company | Nicky Grist | Ford Focus RS WRC01 | 4 | Y4FMC |
| **2002** | | | | | | | | | |
| | Monte Carlo Rally | MC | 18-20/01 | 4th | Ford Motor Company | Nicky Grist | Ford Focus RS WRC02 | 5 | Y5FMC |
| | Swedish Rally | S | 31/01 - 3/02 | 6th | Ford Motor Company | Nicky Grist | Ford Focus RS WRC02 | 5 | Y129XEV |
| | Tour de Corse | F | 8-10/03 | Ret | Ford Motor Company | Nicky Grist | Ford Focus RS WRC02 | 5 | Y5FMC |
| | Rally Catalunya | E | 21-24/03 | 6th | Ford Motor Company | Nicky Grist | Ford Focus RS WRC02 | 5 | EK51HXZ |
| | Cyprus Rally | CY | 19-21/04 | 6th | Ford Motor Company | Nicky Grist | Ford Focus RS WRC02 | 5 | Y129XEV |
| | Rally Argentina | RA | 16-19/05 | 3rd | Ford Motor Company | Nicky Grist | Ford Focus RS WRC02 | 5 | EX02OBB |
| | Acropolis Rally | GR | 14-16/06 | 1st | Ford Motor Company | Nicky Grist | Ford Focus RS WRC02 | 5 | X7FMC |
| | Safari Rally | EAK | 11-14/07 | 1st | Ford Motor Company | Nicky Grist | Ford Focus RS WRC02 | 5 | EK51HYZ |
| | Rally Finland | SF | 8-11/08 | Ret | Ford Motor Company | Nicky Grist | Ford Focus RS WRC02 | 5 | EX02OBE |
| | Deutschland Rally | D | 23-25/08 | 4th | Ford Motor Company | Nicky Grist | Ford Focus RS WRC02 | 5 | EX02OBB |
| | ASCAR - Rockingham | GB | 13-14/09 | 6th | Bintcliffe Motorsport | / | Ford Taurus | | / |
| | Sanremo Rally | I | 19-22/09 | 8th | Ford Motor Company | Nicky Grist | Ford Focus RS WRC02 | 5 | EX02OBE |
| | Rally New Zealand | NZ | 3-6/10 | Ret | Ford Motor Company | Nicky Grist | Ford Focus RS WRC02 | 5 | EX02OBB |
| | Rally Australia | AUS | 31/10 - 3/11 | Ret | Ford Motor Company | Derek Ringer | Ford Focus RS WRC02 | 5 | EX02OBE |
| | Rally of Great Britain | GB | 14-17/11 | 5th | Ford Motor Company | Derek Ringer | Ford Focus RS WRC02 | 5 | EX02OBB |
| **2003** | | | | | | | | | |
| | Monte Carlo Rally | MC | 24-26/01 | 2nd | Citroën Total | Derek Ringer | Citroën Xsara WRC | 17 | 15DDM92 |
| | Swedish Rally | S | 7-9/02 | 5th | Citroën Total | Derek Ringer | Citroën Xsara WRC | 17 | 26CSP92 |
| | Rally of Turkey | TR | 27/02 - 2/03 | 4th | Citroën Total | Derek Ringer | Citroën Xsara WRC | 17 | 14DDM92 |
| | Rally New Zealand | NZ | 10-13/04 | Ret | Citroën Total | Derek Ringer | Citroën Xsara WRC | 17 | 18DDM92 |
| | Rally Argentina | RA | 8-11/05 | Ret | Citroën Total | Derek Ringer | Citroën Xsara WRC | 17 | 28CSP92 |
| | Acropolis Rally | GR | 5-8/06 | 8th | Citroën Total | Derek Ringer | Citroën Xsara WRC | 17 | 21DDM92 |
| | Cyprus Rally | CY | 20-22/06 | 4th | Citroën Total | Derek Ringer | Citroën Xsara WRC | 17 | 14DDM92 |
| | Deutschland Rally | D | 24-27/07 | 4th | Citroën Total | Derek Ringer | Citroën Xsara WRC | 17 | 26CSP92 |
| | Rally Finland | SF | 7-10/08 | Ret | Citroën Total | Derek Ringer | Citroën Xsara WRC | 17 | 22DDM92 |
| | Rally Australia | AUS | 4-7/09 | 4th | Citroën Total | Derek Ringer | Citroën Xsara WRC | 17 | 18DDM92 |
| | Sanremo Rally | I | 3-5/10 | 6th | Citroën Total | Derek Ringer | Citroën Xsara WRC | 17 | 15DDM92 |
| | Tour de Corse | F | 17-19/10 | 5th | Citroën Total | Derek Ringer | Citroën Xsara WRC | 17 | 26CSP92 |
| | Rally Catalunya | E | 23-26/10 | 9th | Citroën Total | Derek Ringer | Citroën Xsara WRC | 17 | 14DDM92 |
| | Rally of Great Britain | GB | 6-9/11 | 4th | Citroën Total | Derek Ringer | Citroën Xsara WRC | 17 | 21DDM92 |
| **2004** | | | | | | | | | |
| | Dakar | | 1-18/01 | 20th | Nissan UK | Tina Thörner | Nissan Pickup 2004 | 202 | PSM428GP |
| | Le Mans 24 Hours | F | 12-13/06 | 9th/3IC | Care Racing | Turner & Rydell | Ferrari 550 Maranello GT1 | 65 | / |
| | UAE Desert Challenge | UAE | 10-15/10 | Ret | Nissan France Dessoude | Tina Thörner | NISSAN Pickup 2003 | 206 | |
| | Baja Portalegre | P | 29-30/10 | 1st | Nissan UK | Tina Thörner | NISSAN Pickup 2005 | 303 | NXR770GP |
| **2005** | | | | | | | | | |
| | Dakar | | 31/12 - 16/01 | Ret | Nissan | Tina Thörner | Nissan Pickup 2005 | 308 | PSM428GP |
| | Killarney Rally of the Lakes | IRL | 29/04 - 01/05 | | McRae Motorsport | | Ford Escort Mk II | 1 | ONM804V |
| | Scottish National Rally | GB | 11/06 | | McRae Motorsport | Nicky Grist | Ford Escort Mk II | 101 | ONM804V |
| | Rally of Great Britain | GB | 15-18/09 | 7th | Škoda Motorsport | Nicky Grist | Skoda Fabia WRC05 | 12 | 3S2 3102 |
| | Rally Australia | AUS | 10-13/11 | Ret | Škoda Motorsport | Nicky Grist | Skoda Fabia WRC05 | 12 | 3S2 3103 |
| **2006** | | | | | | | | | |
| | Porsche SuperCup Nurburgring | D | 7/05 | Ret | Morellato Stars Team | / | Porsche 911 GT3 Cup | 18 | / |
| | Pirelli National Rally | GB | 13/05 | Ret | McRae Motorsport | Nicky Grist | Ford Escort Mk II | 201 | ONM804V |
| | Porsche SuperCup Monaco | MC | 27/05 | 10th | Morellato Stars Team | / | Porsche 911 GT3 Cup | 18 | / |
| | Donegal National Rally | IRL | 16-18/06 | 1st | McRae Motorsport | Nicky Grist | MG Metro 6R4 | 3 | D165WVX |
| | X Games | USA | 3-6/08 | 2nd | Vermont SportsCar | Nicky Grist | Subaru Impreza | 7 | |
| | Knockhill | GB | 2/09 | Ret | Vertu | / | Porsche 997 GT3 Cup | 43 | / |
| | Knockhill | GB | 3/09 | Ret | Vertu | / | Porsche 997 GT3 Cup | 43 | / |
| | Rally Turkey | TR | 13-15/10 | Ret | Kronos Total Citroën WRC | Nicky Grist | Citroën Xsara WRC | 1 | 829DPT78 |
| **2007** | | | | | | | | | |
| | Manx National Rally | GB | 11-12/05 | | McRae Motorsport | Campbell Roy | Ford Escort Mk II | 11 | ONM804V |
| | Baja Aragon | E | 19-22/07 | 2nd | AlgoDyne Green Power RT | Tina Thörner | X-Raid BMW X3CC | 6 | GG-XR 333 |
| | X Games | USA | 2-5/08 | Ret | Vermont SportsCar | Carolyn Bosley | Subaru Impreza | 7 | EFC965 |

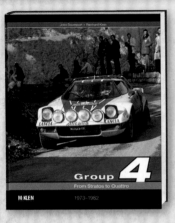